Cisco ASA
for Accidental
Administrators®

Version 1.1

Cisco ASA for Accidental Administrators®

An Illustrated Step-by-Step Cisco ASA Learning and Configuration Guide

Version 1.1

Don R. Crawley
Linux+ and IPv6 Silver Engineer

Seattle, Washington
www.soundtraining.net

Special discounts are available on bulk quantities of soundtraining.net books. For details, contact soundtraining.net, a division of Jonan, Limited, PO Box 48094, Seattle, WA 98148.

Telephone: (206) 988-5858

Email: info@soundtraining.net

Website: www.soundtraining.net

Cover and interior design by Jason Sprenger, Fourth Cup Print and Web Design, Overland Park, Kansas
Back cover photograph: JMC Photography, Seattle, Washington

Reasonable attempts have been made to ensure the accuracy of the information contained in this publication as of the date on which it was written. This publication is distributed in the hope that it will be helpful, but with no guarantees. There are no guarantees made as to the accuracy, reliability, or applicability of this information for any task or purpose whatsoever.

The author recommends that these procedures be used only as a guide to configuration of computers and/or devices in a test environment prior to usage in a production environment. Under no circumstances should these procedures be used in a live, production environment without first being tested in a laboratory environment to determine their suitability, their accuracy, and any security implications.

ISBN: 978-0-9836607-5-0

PO Box 48094
Seattle, Washington 98148-0094
United States of America
On the web: www.soundtraining.net
On the phone: (206) 988-5858
Email: info@soundtraining.net

In memory of Cleo. Sit Cleo, sit.

"Technology, like art, is a soaring exercise of the human imagination."

—Daniel Bell
The Winding Passage

Contents

CHAPTER 2:
Backing Up and Restoring Configurations and Software Images

CHAPTER 3:
Sending Logging Output to a Syslog Server

CHAPTER 4:
Remote Management Options

CHAPTER 8:
Virtual Private Networking (VPNs)

CHAPTER 9:
De-Militarized Zones (DMZs)

CHAPTER 10:
Filtering Content

CHAPTER 11:
Configuring Transparent Mode

POSTLUDE

APPENDICES

INDEX

Prelude

Thank you for purchasing this book. I wrote it for people who, like me, need a clear and understandable guide for learning about and configuring network devices. You will find many practical exercises with lots of step-by-step instructions. This book, like my seminars and workshops, is designed to get you up and running in a minimal amount of time with a minimal amount of theory and background information. In my own work, I often just need something to get me "over the hump" and then I can figure things out. If you are like me in that regard, then this book is for you.

Some background notes:

- I refer frequently to your management workstation in the book. That means the computer you are using to configure and manage the security appliance. I assume, for the purposes of the book, that your computer is running a Windows operating system, but most of the exercises, particularly those using the command-line interface, should work perfectly well with computers running OSX, Unix, or Linux.

- The exercises in this book require a variety of tools and resources, all of which are freely available on the public Internet. To make things as simple as possible, I've provided website URLs where you can download the necessary tools. I have included Google's public DNS servers (8.8.8.8 and 8.8.4.4) when DNS configuration is required. Your default gateway is probably the router between you and the Internet, but I assume, if you are configuring a network security appliance, that you know what a default gateway is and how to determine your gateway.

- This book is written for Cisco's commercial-grade security devices known as the ASA Security Appliances. It is not relevant for Cisco's consumer-grade devices formerly sold under the Linksys brand.

- This book is based primarily on ASA software version 9.0(4) and 9.2(2)4. Most of the configurations should work with any software version 8.3 or later. I've included a couple of notes about how to configure older versions such as 8.2(5), but this book is not really written for older versions.

- Most of the exercises and screen captures are from an ASA 5505. I have also performed these procedures on other ASAs including a 5510, 5512X, and a 5540. The steps in the book are relevant for other ASAs with minor changes, often related to interface configuration, as long as the software versions are similar.

- Most software vendors update their software frequently. Cisco is no exception. With software updates come changes in configuration procedures. Usually such changes are minor, but occasionally they are significant, as in the changes to NAT configuration with version 8.3(1). As mentioned above, this book was written mainly using ASA software version 9.0(4) and 9.2(2)4. Most of the procedures will probably work as written on upcoming software releases. If you are using a different version, be prepared to adapt to changes in configuration procedures. As with all Cisco software, the question mark is often your best friend.

I noticed, once, when it was time for student exercises in a hands-on workshop I attended, that all of us in the class just jumped right into the exercise without reading through the steps first. I realized that, if I took a moment to read through the exercise instructions before beginning, that my understanding and retention improved dramatically. Give yourself the gift of reading through the exercise steps before you begin. I also encourage you to check off each step to ensure you don't miss any of the steps.

As with many things related to information systems and technology, Google (or any search engine) can be a great friend, but do not trust it. Always test solutions in your lab before deploying them in production. Always make backups before making changes.

Be sure to check out your local Cisco users groups. You'll find a wealth of information and great camaraderie. When my schedule permits, I attend the Seattle Cisco Users Group meetings (www.seacug.com).

Toastmasters (www.toastmasters.org) founder, Dr. Ralph C. Smedley, said, "We learn best in moments of enjoyment." Bearing that in mind, enjoy the learning experience and take great satisfaction in knowing that you are helping your end users work more productively, efficiently, and creatively!

About soundtraining.net

soundtraining.net is a Seattle-based publishing and training company that provides learning resources for the IT community. soundtraining.net's customers include CIOs, CTOs, network administrators, network engineers, support desk personnel, and anyone involved in computers and network design, installation, operation, and maintenance. soundtraining.net specializes in Cisco and Linux product training, plus workplace skills books, videos, and training for IT professionals.

Among the training topics offered by soundtraining.net are:

- Cisco ASA Security Appliance Training: Installing, Configuring, Optimizing, and Troubleshooting

- Cisco Router Fundamentals 2-Day Hands On Workshop

- Networking Fundamentals

- Linux Server Training: Installing, Configuring, Optimizing, and Troubleshooting

- Customer Service Training for IT Professionals

Please call or email for information about programs not listed.

soundtraining.net programs are available for presentation onsite, at your location, at your convenience. Call **(206) 988-5858** or email onsite@soundtraining.net.

Additionally, soundtraining.net provides a variety of videos on our video channel at www.soundtraining.net/videos.

Acknowledgements

To produce any book is a huge undertaking. This one is no exception. Thanks to Janet my wife, to the thousands of students worldwide who have challenged me to try to stay ahead of them (I haven't always succeeded), Paul Senness, and the many other friends and family members who deserve to be mentioned in appreciation for their inspiration and support, but in the interest of space, will just have to know how much I love and appreciate them.

Support

I maintain a YouTube channel with a playlist devoted to the Cisco ASA Security Appliance. Many of the procedures in this book have supporting videos. The YouTube channel is www.youtube.com/soundtraining. You'll find the playlist at http://www.youtube.com/playlist?list=PL84F4575D9FB028ED.

Support for the concepts in this book is also available in numerous online forums, including https://supportforums.cisco.com. You will find the forum members to be very knowledgeable and helpful. Such forums are your best choice for online support.

I maintain a Facebook page where I'm sometimes available to answer questions. You'll find it at www.facebook.com/soundtraining.net.

If you require one-on-one support, Cisco offers support contracts which they call SMARTnet. SMARTnet contracts are priced based on the type of equipment you have and the level of support you require. At the time of this writing (Winter 2014/2015), they're very affordable for a Cisco ASA 5505. Just as a point of reference, as I was writing this, I looked up the price of a SMARTnet extended service agreement for a 5505 with a 10 user license at CDW. It was priced at US$71.99 for a one-year contract.

I am not able to provide individual one-on-one support.

Errata

No matter how many times we go over a book before publication, we inevitably discover errors after publication or Cisco changes some procedures or commands. I maintain an errata page for my books at http://www.soundtraining.net/bookstore/errata. If you notice an error, please let me know. My email address is don@soundtraining.net.

Reviews

I'm a small, independent author and publisher. Reviews are incredibly important in helping me compete successfully with the big publishers. If you find this book helpful, please leave a review.

Thank you.

CHAPTER 1:
Understanding Firewall Fundamentals

"Don't anthropomorphize computers—they hate it"

—Unknown

What do firewalls do?

The term firewall is often used, but not well understood by many people. A firewall can be either a hardware device or software implemented on a host computer. At its most fundamental level, a firewall is a means of controlling traffic into or out of a system or a network. The most basic firewalls, such as consumer cable modem firewalls, allow traffic to exit the network, but prevent external traffic from entering the network.

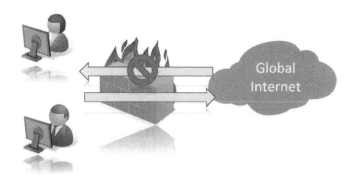

Figure 1: Basic firewall functionality prevents hosts on the Public Internet from initiating connections to hosts in the LAN, but LAN users are able to initiate connections to hosts on the Public Internet

Commercial firewalls, however, are considerably more sophisticated than consumer firewalls.

Service provided by commercial firewalls include:

- Control and manage network traffic
- Access authentication
- Serve as an "in-between"
- Organizational resource protection (including intrusion detection and prevention)
- Monitor, log, and report on events
- VPN concentrator

Types of Firewalls

- **Desktop or personal firewalls**. Desktop or personal firewalls are usually software applications installed on individual computers and which are designed to protect only that particular computer or host. They are often referred to as *host-based firewalls*. Examples include:
  - Windows Defender, which is built in to new versions of Microsoft Windows and available for download for older versions (windows.microsoft.com/en-us/windows/security-essentials-download)
  - ZoneAlarm (www.zonealarm.com)
  - Comodo (www.comodo.com/home/internet-security/firewall.php)
  - Norton Internet Security (us.norton.com/internet-security/)
  - McAfee Personal Firewall (www.mcafee.com)

- **Network firewalls**. Network firewalls are usually purpose-built devices (although there are software applications designed as network firewalls) installed at ingress and egress points in a computer network. Network firewalls are designed to protect multiple hosts within a network and to provide varying levels of protection. The Cisco ASA Security Appliance is an example of a network firewall. Others include:

  - Baracuda (www.barracuda.com/products/firewall)

  - CheckPoint (www.checkpoint.com)

  - Fortinet (www.fortinet.com/)

  - Juniper (www.juniper.net/us/en/products-services/security)

  - McAfee Firewall Enterprise (www.mcafee.com/us/products/firewall-enterprise.aspx)

  - Palo Alto Networks (www.paloaltonetworks.com)

  - Dell SonicWall (www.sonicwall.com)

  - Sophos (www.sophos.com/)

  - WatchGuard (www.watchguard.com)

To learn more about enterprise firewalls, search on the term "gartner magic quadrant enterprise network firewalls).

Certainly, small business and consumer-grade firewalls such as those from LinkSys, NetGear, D-Link, and similar companies also qualify as network firewalls.

Soundthinking Point:
Are desktop firewalls really necessary?

Depending on the research, between 35% and 75% of computer attacks come from internal hosts. Network firewalls cannot protect systems against attacks originating internally. Best practice is to use both network firewalls at critical ingress and egress points and desktop firewalls on all hosts. If you're concerned about the added workload of managing multiple desktop firewalls, learn to work with tools such as Microsoft Group Policy to centralize firewall management.

Classification of Firewalls

The classification of firewalls is based on the layers of the OSI Reference Model[1].

Type of Firewall	Description
Static packet-filtering Operates at OSI layer 3	Static packet-filtering firewalls are first-generation devices that examine data packets at OSI layer 3, based on pre-configured rules.
Circuit-level Operates at OSI layer 4	These second-generation firewalls validate that a packet is either a connection request or part of a connection between two peers at the transport layer.
Application-layer Operates at OSI layers 3, 4, 5, and 7	Application Layer Firewalls, also called Application Layer Proxies, offer the highest level of security by examining traffic at all seven layers of the OSI model, but can add latency.
Dynamic packet-filtering Operates at OSI layers 3, 4, and 5	These firewalls, also known as stateful firewalls, monitor the actual communication process by maintaining a state table. Packets that are part of an existing session (or state) are permitted to pass. The ASA is a stateful firewall.
Transparent Firewalls Operate at OSI layer 2	These firewalls do not have IP addresses, except for a management interface. They are easy to add to an existing network and they filter and inspect traffic flows based on pre-configured rules and interface security levels.

Table 1: The classification of firewalls

Need a refresher on the OSI Reference Model?

Check out my video at http://youtu.be/sVDwG2RdJho.

[1] The Open Systems Interconnection model is a seven-layer model that describes the flow of data from an application on one computer across a network to another application on another computer

Firewall Spectrum

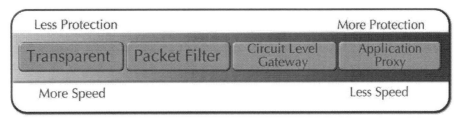

Figure 2: The firewall spectrum

Firewalls that operate at higher layers allow more finely-grained filtering and control, but tend to introduce more latency into network traffic flows. Firewalls that operate at lower layers of the OSI Reference Model allow fewer filtering and control options, but tend to operate with less latency.

Stateful Inspection

All traffic is inspected by the Adaptive Security Algorithm as it passes through the appliance and is either permitted or denied.

Simple packet filters can check for the correct source and destination address and ports, but won't check for correct packet sequence or flags.

Filters also check each packet against the filter, which can introduce latency.

Stateful firewalls like the Cisco ASA Security Appliance consider the state of a packet: Is this a new connection or an established connection?

New connections require the appliance to check the packet against any access-control lists and perform other checks to decide whether to permit or deny the packet.

Established Connections

If a connection is already established, re-checking packets is not required. Most matching packets travel through the fast path in both directions. The fast path performs the following tasks:

- Session lookup
- TCP sequence number check
- IP checksum verification
- Network Address Translations based on existing sessions
- Layer 3 and 4 header adjustments

Adaptive Security Algorithm

The Adaptive Security Algorithm is at the heart of Cisco security appliances. It provides the stateful connection aspects of Cisco security appliance's operation. It creates the *state table*, which is a stateful session flow table. The state table contains connection information such as source and destination addresses. As traffic enters the appliance, it references the state table to determine whether to allow or drop the traffic. Additionally, the ASA generates random TCP sequence numbers for outbound traffic to inhibit the ability of an attacker to hijack a session.

An Overview of Cisco Security Appliances

Cisco introduced the ASA line of security appliances in May of 2005. The ASA combines functionality from the PIX, VPN 3000 concentrator series, and IDS product lines. Through version 7 of the software, the PIX and ASA used the same software. Beginning with version 8, the software was split with different software images for each hardware platform.

The ASA family ranges from the ASA 5505 small office/home office appliance to the ASA 5585-X enterprise security appliance.

Cisco Small Office and Branch Office ASA Security Appliances

ASA 5505

- SOHO security appliance
- 512 MB RAM
- Stateful inspection throughput max: Up to 150 Mbps
- 64 MB minimum system flash
- 8 10/100 Ethernet ports
- Up to 25,000 maximum connections

ASA 5510

The ASA 5510 Security Appliance is no longer available for sale, as of September 16, 2013 and will no longer supported by Cisco as of September 30, 2018. I'm including the data on the 5510 because many organizations will continue to use it for the foreseeable future.

- SMB firewall and VPN solution
- Stateful inspection throughput max: Up to 300 Mbps
- 1.6 GHz Celeron processor
- Default shipping RAM (as of February 2010): 1 GB
- 64 MB minimum system flash
- 4 10/100 Ethernet ports
- 1 10/100 Management port
- Up to five security contexts
- Up to 100 VLANs
- Up to 250 IPSec VPN peers
- Up to 250 SSL VPN peers
- Up to 64,000 concurrent connections

ASA 5512-X

- Stateful inspection throughput (max): 1 Gbps
- Multicore, enterprise-grade processor
- 4 GB RAM
- 4 GB system flash
- Integrated gigabit Ethernet ports: 6 (expandable up to 12)
- Dedicated gigabit Ethernet management port: 1
- Up to 250 IPSec VPN peers
- 2 AnyConnect VPN peers are included, expandable up to 250
- Up to 50 VLANs
- Up to 100,000 concurrent connections

ASA 5515-X

- Stateful inspection throughput (max): 1.2 Gbps
- Multicore, enterprise-grade processor
- 8 GB RAM
- 8 GB system flash
- Integrated gigabit Ethernet ports: 6 (expandable up to 12)
- Dedicated gigabit Ethernet management port: 1
- Up to 5 security contexts
- Up to 250 IPSec VPN peers
- 2 AnyConnect VPN peers are included, expandable up to 250
- Up to 100 VLANs
- Up to 250,000 concurrent connections

Cisco Internet Edge and Enterprise Data Center ASA Security Appliances

For more demanding applications, Cisco offers the ASA 5525-X, ASA 5545-X, ASA 5555-X, and the ASA 5585-X models offering stateful inspection maximum throughput of up to 50 Gbps, up to 350,000 connections per second, up to 10,000,000 concurrent sessions, and up to 10,000 VPN connections, depending on model and license.

Memory on the Cisco ASA Security Appliance

There are three types of memory on the Cisco ASA Security Appliance.

Flash memory is where the software image, configuration files, and other files are stored. You can think of flash memory as being similar to a computer's hard drive. Flash memory exists as a single compact flash card on the Cisco ASA 5505. This memory is also referred to as disk0. Other ASAs support two compact flash cards (internal and external). You can view the contents of flash memory with the command *show flash* or *show disk*. If you have a larger ASA, you can specify which flash memory card's contents to view by appending a number to the *show disk* command, such as *show disk1*.

SDRAM (Synchronous Dynamic Random Access Memory) is where the devices loads the software image, configuration files, and other files for use during operation. The files are loaded into SDRAM at startup. SDRAM exists as DIMM (Dual In-Line Memory Module) sticks. As of this writing, the recommended SDRAM size for an ASA 5505 is 512MB. You can view the current configuration as it exists in SDRAM with the command *show running-config*, which most people abbreviate to *show run*.

ROM (Read-Only Memory) stores the system bootstrap and files used for repairs and diagnostics. If you need to perform password recovery procedures, such as when you have forgotten the administrator password, you will boot the system in ROM Monitor (ROMMON) mode. ROMMON is also used when the ASA's software image becomes corrupted or accidentally erased. Later in this chapter, in the section on password recovery, you will learn one aspect of working in ROMMON.

The Cisco ASA 5505 Chassis

The Front Panel

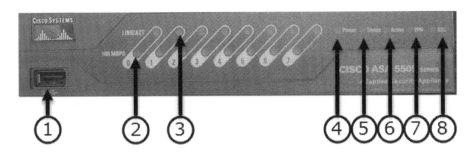

Figure 3: The front panel of an ASA 5505

1	USB 2.0 (Reserved for future use)	5	**Flashing green:** Booting **Solid green:** Booted **Amber:** Error
2	100 Mbps	6	**Green:** Unit is forwarding traffic **Amber:** Unit is on standby (as part of a high-availability setup)
3	Link Activity	7	**Solid green:** VPN tunnel is established **Flashing green:** VPN tunnel is being initiated **Amber:** VPN tunnel failed to initiate
4	Unit is receiving power	8	Security Services Card slot is occupied

The Rear Panel

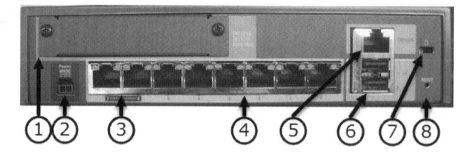

Figure 4:
The rear panel
of a 5505

1	Security Services Card (SSC) slot	5	Serial console cable port for managing the device in the command-line interface
2	Power connector	6	USB 2.0 (reserved for future use)
3	Ethernet ports e6 and e7 are Fast Ethernet ports (100 Mbps) and are PoE (Power over Ethernet) enabled	7	Security lock slot
4	Ports e0 through e5 are also Fast Ethernet ports (100 Mbps), but are not PoE enabled	8	Reset button (reserved for future use)

Controlling the Appliance from its Serial Cable Console Interface

The ASA's console port is connected to your management workstation (the computer you use to manage the security appliance) for monitoring and configuration by a light blue console cable. The console cable is included with all Cisco devices and provides a serial connection from your PC's serial port (using a DB-9 connector) to your device's console port (using an RJ-45 connector). You can then use any terminal emulation software to connect to the console port of your device to view console output and issue console configuration commands. The terminal emulation software which I've used for years and recommend is PuTTY, available for free at www.putty.org. Other terminal emulation software includes TeraTerm (http://ttssh2.sourceforge.jp/index.html.en) and SecureCRT (http://www.vandyke.com/products/securecrt/). Windows computers before Windows Vista include HyperTerminal which can also be used for serial console and Telnet connections. The console cable does not allow network functionality. You can manage your ASA through four different techniques: the console connection, a Telnet connection, a Secure Shell (SSH) connection, or the Adaptive Security Device Manager (ASDM)). In most of the exercises in this book, you will use the serial cable console connection or the ASDM.

Connect the DB9 connector to the serial port on your management workstation and the RJ45 connector goes into the port marked Console on the back of your firewall. Be careful, it's easy to get confused and plug the console cable into an Ethernet port. Don't do that!

Figure 5:
An official Cisco serial console cable,
photo by Paul R. Senness

If your management workstation does not have a DB9 serial connector, you must use a USB-to-Serial adapter.

Once you install it, you'll also need to know which comm port it is using. The easiest way to do that is to check under Devices and Printers where you should see it, along with an indication of which comm port it was assigned. You may need to scroll to the bottom of the window to see it.

Figure 6:
A USB-to-Serial adapter dongle,
photo by Paul R. Senness

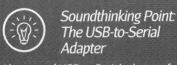

Soundthinking Point: The USB-to-Serial Adapter

I have used USB-to-Serial adapters from three separate manufacturers. In two cases, my experience was painful. Two of the adapters frequently caused my laptop to bluescreen. It later turned out that certain chipsets perform better at this than others. I found a website which specializes in such adapters and found one that was Windows logo certified, based on its chipset, which has been trouble-free. Be careful about which one you buy. Some of the cheaper adapters include poorly written drivers which don't work well with modern operating systems. Expect to spend $35 to $40 on a good adapter. I've had good luck getting adapters from *www.usconverters.com*.

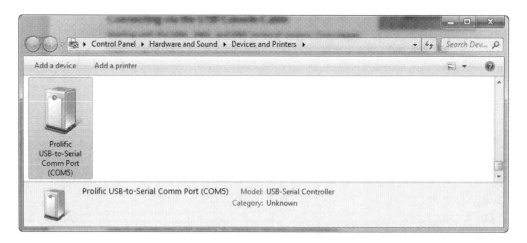

Figure 7: Viewing devices connected to a computer running Windows 7

Notice in the screen capture that my computer assigned the adapter to comm port 5 (COM5). You can also look under the Device Manager to see which port it's using.

Navigating in the Cisco Command Line

Much of your work on Cisco devices will be done in the command line. Here are some tips to help you work in the Cisco command line environment:

Command Modes

The Cisco command interpreter is called EXEC. While working in EXEC, there are several modes, indicated by the prompt. Each mode offers its own set of unique commands.

- User Mode: The prompt is the hostname followed by a greater-than symbol (>). You can think of user mode as a read-only mode. There are very few commands available in user mode and, frankly, you probably won't use it very much.

Figure 8: User mode prompt

- Privileged Mode: The prompt is the hostname followed by a hash mark, also referred to as a pound sign (#). You can get to privileged mode from user mode by typing the command *enable*, which most people abbreviate to *en*. In privileged mode you have access to all commands and command modes.

```
ciscoasa>
ciscoasa> enable
Password:
ciscoasa#
```

Figure 9: The privileged mode prompt

- Global Configuration Mode: The prompt is the hostname followed by (config)#. You get to global configuration mode by typing the command *configure terminal*, which most people abbreviate to *conf t*. In global configuration mode, you can make changes to the device's configuration. You can navigate to other modes such as interface configuration mode or tunnel configuration mode from global configuration mode.

Figure 10:
A global configuration mode prompt

```
ciscoasa#
ciscoasa# configure terminal
ciscoasa(config)#
```

You can go back to a higher mode by typing *exit*. You can go all the way back to privileged mode by touching the key combination of Ctrl+Z.

Unlike a Cisco router, the ASA allows you to enter higher level commands while working in sub-command modes.

When you use a *show* command to display, say, a long configuration file, the device will show a single page at a time with a <--- More ---> prompt at the bottom of the page. You can show the next line by pressing the Enter key or the next page by pressing the Space Bar. You can exit from the display by pressing the Q key.

Getting Help in the Command Line

Like most Cisco commercial-grade devices, help is available at the command line by simply entering a question mark. Suppose you want to know all the commands available in a particular mode. Simply enter a question mark and the ASA will show you everything that's available. For example, in the following screen capture, I'm in user mode (denoted by a ">" prompt) and, when I enter a question mark, the device shows a fairly small list of available commands:

```
asa01>
asa01> ?

  clear         Reset functions
  enable        Turn on privileged commands
  exit          Exit from the EXEC
  help          Interactive help for commands
  login         Log in as a particular user
  logout        Exit from the EXEC
  no            Negate a command or set its defaults
  ping          Send echo messages
  quit          Exit from the EXEC
  show          Show running system information
  traceroute    Trace route to destination
asa01>
asa01>
```

Figure 11:
Getting help in general

Notice that one of the available commands is *show*. You can also enter a command such as *show*, followed by a question mark to see the available subcommands for use with show, as seen in the next screen capture:

```
asa01>
asa01> show ?

  checksum     Display configuration information cryptochecksum
  curpriv      Display current privilege level
  disk0:       Display information about disk0: file system
  flash:       Display information about flash: file system
  history      Display the session command history
  inventory    Show all inventory information for all slots
  power        Power attributes
  version      Display system software version
asa01> show
```

Figure 12:
Getting
help for
a specific
command

Additionally, you can type the first letter of a command with a question mark to see all the available commands which start with that particular letter:

Figure 13:
Getting help for commands
which start with a specific letter

```
                   --
asa01>
asa01> show c?

  checksum      curpriv
asa01> show c
```

Finally, if you mistype a command, the software displays a caret at the point where it no longer understands the command. In the following screen capture, I mistyped the word *version* so you can see the output in that situation:

```
asa01>
asa01> show verson
                  ^
ERROR: % Invalid input detected at '^' marker.
asa01>
```

Notice the caret under the letter *o*. The ASA is saying, "I understand everything up through *vers*, but the *o* doesn't make any sense to me." I could type the partial command show *vers?* to see all options for completing the command.

Help in the ASDM

When working in the ASDM, context-aware HTML-based help is available by clicking the question mark in the menu bar at the top of the manager.

Command Shorthand Abbreviation

The ASA, like other Cisco devices, supports command shorthand abbreviations. You simply have to type enough of the command so it's unique and can't be anything else. For example, you can abbreviate *show version* with *sh ve*. Another common abbreviation is, instead of typing the lengthy command *show running-config*, to type simply *sh ru*. It's also common to type *en* instead of *enable* when moving into privileged mode and *conf t* instead of *configure terminal* when moving into global configuration mode.

Password Recovery

The term *password recovery* is somewhat misleading. A more accurate term would be *emergency password resetting*. The administrative password(s) are encrypted and cannot be recovered. However, they can be reset to a new, known value. Even though it would more accurately be called *emergency password resetting*, Cisco refers to the procedure as *password recovery*, so for the purpose of this document, I will also call it *password recovery*. Password recovery procedures are used when it is necessary to administer a Cisco device and the administrator password(s) are not known. Password recovery procedures on the Cisco ASA security appliance are similar to the procedures used on a Cisco router.

Password Recovery on the ASA Security Appliance

Use the following procedures to perform password recovery on a Cisco ASA security appliance:

1. Power cycle the appliance

2. Interrupt the boot process to enter ROM Monitor mode

3. Change the configuration register value to 0x41 which prevents the appliance from reading the stored configuration in flash memory on boot

4. Reboot the appliance

5. The saved configuration is ignored, therefore no configuration is present and no password(s) are required to enter privileged mode

6. Enter privileged mode

7. Copy the stored configuration from flash into the appliance's operating memory

8. Change the password(s) to known values

9. Disable user authentication (if necessary)

10. Save the configuration to flash memory

11. Change the configuration register back to the default of 0x01

12. Reload the appliance

ASA Software Version

As mentioned previously, this book and its exercises are based primarily on ASA software versions 9.0(4) and 9.2(2)4. Use the command show version to identify the software version installed on your ASA. Substantial changes were introduced in software version 8.3x. If your ASA is running a software version numbered 8.2x or lower, some of the commands shown may not work. See later sections of the book for information on upgrading to a more recent software version.

Hands-On Exercise 1.1:
Connecting to the Security Appliance's Console Port

In this exercise, you will begin the process of configuring your firewall from scratch. You will use password recovery procedures to reset the password to a known value, you will record important information about the firewall, and you will then erase the configuration and build a new configuration from scratch.

Exercise Diagram

For this exercise, you will connect your management workstation to the ASA security appliance using the serial console cable. If your management workstation does not have a DB9 serial connector, you must use a USB-to-serial converter, along with the console cable. It is not necessary to connect to a network for this exercise.

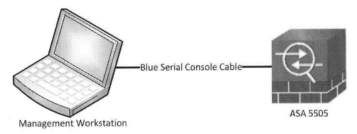

Exercise Requirements:

- ASA Security Appliance

- A management workstation with terminal emulation software such as PuTTY terminal emulation software, available for free from www.putty.org

- Console cable with a DB-9 serial connector on one end and an RJ45 connector on the other. Cisco includes console cables with the ASA Security Appliance. If yours is missing, you can purchase one or make one. There are many guides available online. Search on the term "how to build a Cisco console cable" and you'll find plenty of guides.

- If your computer doesn't have a serial port, as mentioned earlier, you'll also need a USB-to-Serial adapter. Again, I've had good luck purchasing adapters from www.usconverters.com.

Exercise Steps

1. Open PuTTY on your PC (Alternatively, you may use any terminal emulation software you wish such as TeraTerm, SecureCRT, or others.): Click on Start, then click on All Programs>PuTTY. Click on the PuTTY application to start the PuTTY application.

2. Configure PuTTY with the following settings:

   Connection type: Serial
   Com port: Set according to the appropriate COM port as indicated previously
   Click "Open"

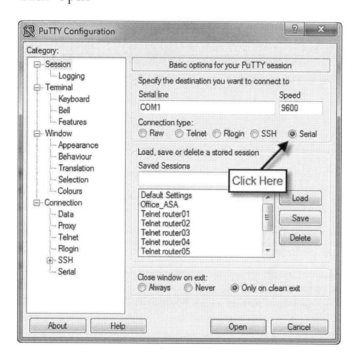

Figure 15:
Opening a serial connection
with PuTTY

(It is not necessary to configure the following settings manually in PuTTY. They are included here as a reference in case you are using a different terminal program: Connect using: COM1 (or whichever COM port you're using to connect), Bits per second: 9600, Data bits: 8, Parity: None, Stop bits: 1, Flow control: None)

3. Press the Enter key and you should see a prompt. (If you have booted your ASA within the last couple of minutes, it may take a moment before text appears in your terminal window. Remember, patience is a virtue.)

Hands-On Exercise 1.2:
Password Recovery on the Security Appliance

This procedure will require you to power-cycle your appliance by unplugging it at the power strip and plugging it back in. You will then interrupt the boot process and change the configuration register to prevent the appliance from reading its stored configuration at boot.

Watch the Video

There is a video on my YouTube channel in which I demonstrate the following procedures. Watch the video at http://youtu.be/DpaIM3-4ZBE.

Exercise Diagram

The diagram is the same as for the previous exercise.

Exercise Prerequisites

The prerequisites are the same as for the previous exercise.

Exercise Steps

1. Power-cycle your appliance by using either power button or, on the ASA 5505 removing and re-inserting the plug at the power strip.

2. When prompted, press Esc to interrupt the boot process and enter ROM Monitor mode. You should immediately see a rommon prompt (rommon #0>). The number following the word *rommon* is just a line number which will increment with each command. You can ignore it.

3. At the rommon prompt, enter the confreg command to view the current configuration register setting:

   ```
   rommon #0>confreg
   ```

4. The current configuration register should be the default of 0x01 (it will actually display as 0x00000001). The security appliance will ask if you want to make changes to the configuration register. Answer no when prompted.

5. You must change the configuration register to 0x41, which tells the appliance to ignore its saved (startup) configuration upon boot:

   ```
   rommon #1>confreg 0x41
   ```

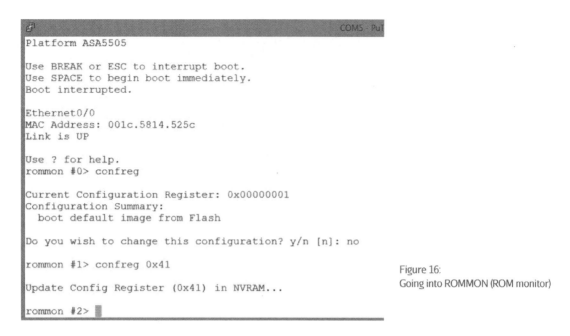

```
Platform ASA5505

Use BREAK or ESC to interrupt boot.
Use SPACE to begin boot immediately.
Boot interrupted.

Ethernet0/0
MAC Address: 001c.5814.525c
Link is UP

Use ? for help.
rommon #0> confreg

Current Configuration Register: 0x00000001
Configuration Summary:
  boot default image from Flash

Do you wish to change this configuration? y/n [n]: no

rommon #1> confreg 0x41

Update Config Register (0x41) in NVRAM...

rommon #2>
```

Figure 16:
Going into ROMMON (ROM monitor)

6. Reset the appliance with the boot command:

   rommon #2>**boot**

7. Notice that the security appliance ignores its startup configuration during the boot process. When it finishes booting, you should see a generic User Mode prompt:

   ciscoasa>

8. If the device asks if you want to pre-configure the firewall through interactive prompts, type **no** and press the Enter key. Enter the enable command to enter Privileged Mode. When the device prompts you for a password, simply press <Enter> (at this point, the password is blank):

   ciscoasa>**enable**

   Password:<Enter> (No password is required because the device has ignored its saved configuration, including the privileged mode password.)

   ciscoasa#

9. Copy the startup configuration file into the running configuration with the following command:

   ciscoasa#**copy startup-config running-config**

   Destination filename [running-config]?<Enter>

10. The previously saved configuration is now the active configuration, but since the security appliance is already in Privileged Mode, privileged access is not disabled. Next, in configuration mode, enter the following command to change the Privileged Mode password to a known value (in this case, we'll use the password *p@ss5678*):

    ciscoasa#**conf t** (The command *conf t* is short for *configure terminal*. Also, the device may ask if you want to enable call-home reporting. Say no for now.)

    ciscoasa(config)#**enable password p@ss5678**

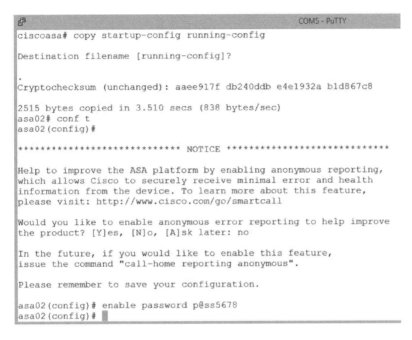

Figure 17:
Copying the saved configuration and changing the privileged mode password

11. Your security appliance may also be configured to support user authentication. You can check it to determine if user authentication is enabled with the following command:

    ciscoasa#**show run aaa**

12. If you see output similar to this, user authentication has been enabled (Note: Not all firewalls will be configured for aaa authentication, nor will all firewalls display all of the following configuration lines):

    ciscoasa#**show run aaa**

    aaa authentication enable console LOCAL

    aaa authentication serial console LOCAL

    aaa authentication ssh console LOCAL

    aaa authorization command LOCAL

    If the command *show run aaa* produces no output, you can skip to step 14.

25

13. In the above output, local user database authentication has been enabled for privileged mode console logons (enable), serial console logons, ssh console logons, and for various levels of commands. In a "real-world" situation, you may or may not want to disable such authentication, but if you do not know the passwords required to access the security appliance, you will have to disable aaa authentication with the following configuration mode commands (and for the purpose of this exercise, please execute the following commands):

```
ciscoasa(config)#no aaa authentication enable console LOCAL
```

```
ciscoasa(config)#no aaa authentication serial console LOCAL
```

```
ciscoasa(config)#no aaa authentication ssh console LOCAL
```

```
ciscoasa(config)#no aaa authorization command LOCAL
```

14. While still in Configuration Mode, reset the configuration register to the default of 0x01 to force the security appliance to read its startup configuration on boot:

```
ciscoasa(config)#config-register 0x01
```

```
ciscoasa(config)#exit
```

```
asa02(config)# config-register 0x01
asa02(config)# exit
asa02#
```

Figure 18:
Resetting the configuration register.

15. Use the following command to view the configuration register setting:

```
ciscoasa#show version
```

16. At bottom of the output of the show version command, you should see the following statement:

```
Configuration register is 0x41 (will be 0x1 at next reload)
```

17. Save the current configuration with the copy run start command to make the above changes persistent:

```
ciscoasa#copy run start
```

```
Source filename [running-config] <Enter>
```

18. Reload the security appliance:

```
ciscoasa# reload
```

```
Proceed with reload? [confirm]<Enter>
```

```
Configuration register is 0x41 (will be 0x1 at next reload)
Configuration last modified by enable_15 at 14:10:08.009 UTC Thu Nov 27 2014
asa02# copy run start

Source filename [running-config]?
Cryptochecksum: 3be754ee f1328dff 02bbc363 c6f40153

3004 bytes copied in 1.240 secs (3004 bytes/sec)
asa02# reload
Proceed with reload? [confirm]
asa02#


***
*** --- START GRACEFUL SHUTDOWN ---
```

Figure 19:
Saving the
configuration
and reloading
the device.

If the device says the configuration has been modified and asks you to save it before reloading, say **yes**.

Erasing the Stored Configuration

Like Cisco routers, an ASA security appliance runs its software image in dynamic RAM and loads its configuration file (the running-config) into RAM at boot. The configuration file is stored in a hidden file in flash memory when the appliance is powered down. To build a system from a pristine state, you must first erase the startup-config file in flash memory.

Hands-On Exercise 1.3:
Removing the Existing Configuration

In this exercise, you will return your ASA to a blank configuration.

1. Log in to the console port on your ASA and enter privileged mode:

    ciscoasa> **en**

    Password: **p@ss5678**

    ciscoasa#

2. Enter the following commands to reset your ASA to a blank configuration:

    ciscoasa# **write erase**

    Erase configuration in flash memory? [confirm]<Enter>

    ciscoasa# **reload**

    Proceed with reload? [confirm]<Enter>

When your ASA finishes reloading, it will ask if you want to pre-configure the firewall through interactive prompts. Type no and press the Enter key.

Some ASA Basics

Before we start building the new configuration, let's go over some basic information about the Cisco ASA. That way, you'll know what you're doing as you enter the setup commands.

Network Address Translation (NAT)

Internet Protocol version 4 is the transport protocol currently in use on the public Internet. It is based on a 32-bit address space which (mathematically) supports approximately 4,000,000,000 hosts (2^{32}). Due to the rapid growth of the Internet since the mid 1990s, the global Internet is now out of public IP addresses (https://www.icann.org/news/announcement-2-2014-05-20-en). Ultimately, it will be necessary to migrate from IPv4 to IPv6, a new protocol which is already widely supported and which is gradually being implemented throughout the world. The Cisco ASA Security Appliance supports IPv6 and I'll add IPv6 support in a future edition of this book. In the meantime, a widely-used temporary solution to help alleviate the crisis in IP addresses is Port Address Translation (PAT), a form of Network Address Translation (NAT). PAT allows multiple private (RFC 1918) addresses to share a single, registered public address.

The private (RFC 1918) addresses are:

- 10.0.0.0/8
- 172.16.0.0/12
- 192.168.0.0/16

On a Cisco security appliance, the internal or private addresses are referred to as *local* addresses and the public addresses (those that are translated) are *global* addresses.

Two forms of NAT are available on a Cisco security appliance: static network address translation and dynamic network address translation.

Static Translation

Static translation creates a one-to-one mapping of local to global addresses. Static translation is most commonly seen when internal hosts need to be accessible to Internet users. Mail servers, Web servers, and FTP servers are all examples of internal hosts that might need to accessible to Internet users.

Dynamic Address Translation

Dynamic address translation (dynamic NAT) translates multiple internal addresses into a single global address or a limited pool of global addresses. Dynamic NAT is also known as Port Address Translation (PAT). Often, when people refer to NAT, they're actually talking about PAT, such as with home networks.

PAT translates multiple internal (local) addresses into a single global address. The source port is changed by the firewall to create a unique connection in spite of the use of a single global address. PAT is limited to approximately 64,000 translations. That corresponds roughly to the number of available TCP/UDP ports, minus some previously assigned ports. Certain applications which require specific source and destination ports may not function with PAT.

Configuring Port Address Translation

For example, to configure port address translation (PAT) in which the 192.168.1.0/24 subnet, connected to the inside interface, is protected behind the address on the outside interface, you would enter the following three statements in global configuration mode:

```
ciscoasa(config)#object network net-192.168.1
ciscoasa(config-network-object)#subnet 192.168.1.0 255.255.255.0
ciscoasa(config-network-object)#nat (inside,outside) dynamic interface
```

As mentioned in an upcoming exercise, many new ASAs ship with older versions of the ASA software. The above configuration is for use with software versions 8.3 and later. If you're running an earlier version of the software, you can either upgrade to a more recent version (this book is based primarily on software version 9.0(4) and 9.2(2)4) or use the procedures indicated in the next text block.

If You Are Using an ASA Software Version Prior to 8.3(1)

Cisco released ASA software version 8.3(1) on March 8, 2010. Version 8.3(1) included many enhancements and new features, plus a major change in the command syntax for configuring port address translation.

Use the command *show version* to identify the software version running on your ASA.

If you're still using a version with a lower number than 8.3(1), two commands are required to configure PAT. The nat command specifies the translation ID, the local IP address range and the network mask. The global command specifies the translation ID (which must match the one used in the nat statement) and the outside IP address and mask that will be shared by the internal hosts.

For example:

```
asa(config)#nat (inside) 10 192.168.1.0 255.255.255.0
asa(config)#global (outside) 10 interface
```

The above configuration allows hosts on the 192.168.1.0/24 network connected to the inside interface to share whatever address is assigned to the outside interface for PAT. You could also configure a specific IP address and mask in the global statement instead of using the *interface* option.

Understanding VLANs and Security Levels

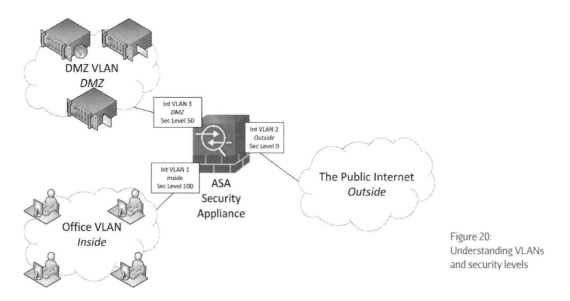

Figure 20:
Understanding VLANs
and security levels

A VLAN is a *virtual local area network*. VLANs consist of one or more administratively assigned physical interfaces on a switch that share a common broadcast domain (a common subnet address). Some Cisco ASA Security Appliances have a limited number of physical interfaces, but when used with VLANs on a switch, hosts can be grouped into separate broadcast domains for security purposes and/or traffic isolation. A common use of VLANs is to create one VLAN for the office, one for a DMZ, and one for an outside interface.

VLAN Tagging

Ethernet frames are tagged with a VLAN identifier that associates the frame with a particular VLAN. Doing so allows traffic for multiple VLANs to pass through a single physical interface.

Security Levels

A fundamental concept in Cisco security appliances is that of security levels. Security levels are assigned to interfaces. Traffic can flow relatively unimpeded from an interface with a higher security level to an interface with a lower security level. In order for traffic to flow from an interface with a lower security level to an interface with a higher security level, access lists and static NAT must be implemented. The default configuration assigns a security level of 100 to the inside interface and a security level of 0 to the outside interface. In fact, when you're configuring interfaces and you give an interface the name *inside*, the security appliance will automatically assign that interface a security level of 100. Similarly, when you assign the name *outside* to an interface, the security appliance will automatically assign that interface a security level of 0. You can name the interfaces anything you wish, but it's common practice to use the names inside for the interface connected to the office LAN and outside for the interface connected to the public Internet.

Assigning Switch Ports to VLANs

On the ASA 5505, the *nameif* command creates a VLAN and the *switchport access* command associates a physical interface with a VLAN. A single IP address can then be assigned to the VLAN interface.

Figure 21:
Assigning switchports to VLANs

```
ciscoasa# conf t
ciscoasa(config)# interface vlan 1
ciscoasa(config-if)# nameif inside
ciscoasa(config-if)# security-level 100
ciscoasa(config-if)# ip address 192.168.101.1
ciscoasa(config-if)# interface ethernet 0/1
ciscoasa(config-if)# switchport access vlan 1
ciscoasa(config-if)# interface ethernet 0/2
ciscoasa(config-if)# switchport access vlan 1
ciscoasa(config-if)#
```

On other ASA security appliances, the *nameif* command is used on physical interfaces such as Ethernet 0/0 and VLANs are created on sub-interfaces. Sub-interfaces allow you to divide physical interfaces into multiple logical interfaces. Such logical interfaces are tagged with different VLAN IDs. Interfaces with one or more VLAN sub-interfaces are automatically tagged as 802.1q trunk interfaces.

This type of VLAN configuration is compatible with 802.1q trunking on a Catalyst switch.

AAA: Authentication, Authorization, and Accounting

The concept of AAA is a thread that runs through many aspects of configuring and operating security appliances. AAA is about knowing who is coming in to a system or network, what that individual is allowed to do, and finally, what they did while they were there.

- Authentication: Who you are
- Authorization: What you are allowed to do
- Accounting: What you did and for how long

AAA can be implemented through a local user database stored on the individual security appliance or it can be implemented through servers using technologies such as RADIUS or TACACS+ for administration and VPN access. The ASA can also implement AAA by connecting to authentication and directory services such as LDAP (Lightweight Directory Access Protocol) and Kerberos for VPN authentication.

Additionally, Cisco offers a hardware solution called Cisco Secure Access Control Server Solution Engine for use in implementing centralized AAA, including RADIUS and TACACS+. For more information, visit http://www.cisco.com/c/en/us/products/security/secure-access-control-server-solution-engine/index.html.

Basics of Encryption Including Single Key and PKI

Single Key Encryption

Single-key encryption is also known as symmetric key cryptography. When single-key encryption is used, both parties to a communication share a key. The same key is used to encrypt the message and to decrypt the message. The obvious problem is that the key has to be transmitted from one party to another and, during the transmission process, is subject to interception by an unintended third party. A non-technical example of single-key encryption is a combination lock on a door. Everyone uses the same combination to open the door. As more people are given the combination, the likelihood of a security breach increases.

PKI (Public Key Infrastructure)

PKI is an acronym for Public Key Infrastructure. It is also known as asymmetric key cryptography. A PKI is the combination of hardware, software, protocols, and policies used to enforce various levels of security.

A PKI is used to ensure confidentiality, authentication, integrity, and non-repudiation. The assurances provided by a PKI are very similar to the basic elements of security discussed earlier. It may help you to remember the concept of CAIN:

Confidentiality

Confidentiality is the assurance that the communication is not being unintentionally disclosed to a third party.

Authentication

Authentication is the assurance that the communication is taking place between the intended parties and that the parties to the communication are indeed who they say they are.

Integrity

Integrity is the assurance that the communication has not been altered in transit.

Non-Repudiation

Non-repudiation is the assurance that one party to a transaction cannot later falsely claim that the transaction did not occur.

How Does a PKI Work?

Two keys are used to create a PKI: a public key and a private key. The two keys are not identical, but they are mathematically related. The public key is available to anyone in the world, however the private key is available only to its owner. Messages encrypted with a public key can only be decrypted with the related private key. Similarly, messages decrypted with a public key could only have been encrypted by the related private key. The private key never leaves its owner.

If you'd like to experiment with PKI, you can get a free digital email signature from Comodo by visiting https://www.comodo.com/home/email-security/free-email-certificate.php. You can also get a free SSL certificate from http://www.startssl.com.

Understanding the Eight Basic Commands on a Cisco ASA Security Appliance

There are literally thousands of commands and sub-commands available to configure a Cisco security appliance. As you gain knowledge of the appliance, you will use more and more of the commands. Initially, however, there are just a few commands required to configure basic functionality on the appliance. Basic functionality is defined as allowing inside hosts to access outside hosts, but not allowing outside hosts to access the inside hosts. Additionally, management must be allowed from at least one inside host. To enable basic functionality, there are eight basic commands:

- interface
- nameif
- security-level
- ip address
- switchport access
- object network
- nat
- route

interface

The interface command identifies either the hardware interface or the Switch Virtual Interface (VLAN interface) that will be configured. Once in interface configuration mode, you can assign physical interfaces to switchports and enable them (turn them on). You can also assign names and security levels to VLAN interfaces.

nameif

The *nameif* command gives the interface a name and assigns a security level. Typical names are *outside*, *inside*, or *DMZ*.

security-level

Security levels are numeric values, ranging from 0 to 100, used by the appliance to control traffic flow. Traffic is permitted to flow from interfaces with higher security levels to interfaces with lower security levels, but not the other way. Access-lists and static NAT must be used to permit traffic to flow from lower security levels to higher security levels. The default security level for an outside interface is 0. For an inside interface, the default security level is 100. In the following sample configuration, the interface command is first used to name the inside and outside VLAN interfaces, then the DMZ interface is named and a security level of 50 is assigned to it.

```
ciscoasa(config)# interface vlan1
ciscoasa(config-if)# nameif inside
INFO: Security level for "inside" set to 100 by default.
ciscoasa(config-if)# interface vlan2
ciscoasa(config-if)# nameif outside
INFO: Security level for "outside" set to 0 by default.
ciscoasa(config-if)# interface vlan3
ciscoasa(config-if)# nameif dmz
ciscoasa(config-if)# security-level 50
```

ip address

The ip address command assigns an IP address to a VLAN interface either statically or by making it a DHCP client. With modern versions of security appliance software, it is not necessary to explicitly configure default subnet masks. If you are using non-standard masks, you must explicitly configure the mask, otherwise, it is not necessary.

In the following sample configuration, an IP address is assigned to VLAN 1, the inside interface.

```
ciscoasa(config-if)# interface vlan 1
ciscoasa(config-if)# ip address 192.168.1.1
```

Configuring interfaces on 55x0 appliances

Notice on the following screen capture from a Cisco ASA 5540 security appliance that the *nameif* command is used to name physical interfaces instead of VLAN interfaces.

```
ciscoasa(config-if)# interface gigabitethernet0/1
ciscoasa(config-if)# speed 1000
ciscoasa(config-if)# duplex full
ciscoasa(config-if)# nameif inside
INFO: Security level for "inside" set to 100 by default.
ciscoasa(config-if)# ip address 10.16.14.1 255.255.255.0
ciscoasa(config-if)# no shutdown
ciscoasa(config-if)#
```

Figure 22:
Naming interfaces
on a larger ASA

switchport access

The switchport access command on the ASA 5505 security appliance assigns a physical interface to a logical (VLAN) interface. In the next example, the interface command is used to identify physical interfaces, assign them to switchports on the appliance, and enable them (turn them on). This command is not used on the ASA 55x0 appliances.

```
ciscoasa(config-if)# interface ethernet 0/0

ciscoasa(config-if)# switchport access vlan 2

ciscoasa(config-if)# no shutdown

ciscoasa(config-if)# interface ethernet 0/1

ciscoasa(config-if)# switchport access vlan 1

ciscoasa(config-if)# no shutdown
```

object network obj_any

The object network obj_any statement creates an object called "obj_any". (You do not have to name the object "obj_any"; that is a descriptive name, but you could just as easily name it "Juan".) The network option states that this particular object will be based on IP addresses. The subnet 0.0.0.0 0.0.0.0 command states that obj_any will affect any IP address not configured on any other object. If no other object has been configured, it will affect all IP addresses.

```
ciscoasa(config-if)#object network obj _ any

ciscoasa(config-network-object)#subnet 0.0.0.0 0.0.0.0
```

nat

The nat statement, as shown below, tells the firewall to allow all traffic flowing from the inside to the outside interface to use dynamic NAT. The *interface* command tells it to use whatever address is configured on the outside interface.

```
ciscoasa(config)#nat (inside,outside) dynamic interface
```

route

The route command, in its most basic form, assigns a default route for traffic, typically to an ISP's router. It can also be used in conjunction with access-lists to send specific types of traffic to specific hosts on specific subnets.

In this sample configuration, the route command is used to configure a default route to the ISP's router at 12.3.4.6. The two zeroes before the ISP's router address are shorthand for an IP address of 0.0.0.0 and a mask of 0.0.0.0. The statement *outside* identifies the interface through which traffic will flow to reach the default route.

```
ciscoasa(config-if)# route outside 0 0 12.3.4.6
```

The above commands create a very basic firewall, however, using a sophisticated device such as a Cisco ASA security appliance to perform such basic firewall functions is in some senses overkill.

Just Beyond the Basics

Other commands to use include *hostname* to identify the firewall, *telnet* or *SSH* to allow remote administration, *DHCPD* commands to allow the firewall to assign IP addresses to inside hosts, and *static NAT* and *access-list* commands to allow internal hosts such as DMZ Web servers or DMZ mail servers to be accessible to Internet hosts. Of course, there are many more advanced commands, many of which you will learn later in this book.

Sample Base Configuration

```
ciscoasa(config)# interface vlan1

ciscoasa(config-if)# nameif inside

INFO: Security level for "inside" set to 100 by default.

ciscoasa(config-if)# interface vlan2

ciscoasa(config-if)# nameif outside

INFO: Security level for "outside" set to 0 by default.

ciscoasa(config-if)# interface ethernet 0/0

ciscoasa(config-if)# switchport access vlan 2

ciscoasa(config-if)# no shutdown

ciscoasa(config-if)# interface ethernet 0/1

ciscoasa(config-if)# switchport access vlan 1

ciscoasa(config-if)# no shutdown

ciscoasa(config-if)# interface vlan 2

ciscoasa(config-if)# ip address dhcp setroute

ciscoasa(config-if)# interface vlan 1

ciscoasa(config-if)# ip address 192.168.1.1

ciscoasa(config-if)# route outside 0 0 12.3.4.6

ciscoasa(config-if)#object network obj _ any

ciscoasa(config-network-object)#subnet 0.0.0.0 0.0.0.0

ciscoasa(config)#nat (inside,outside) dynamic interface

ciscoasa(config)#exit
```

Configuring NAT Prior to Software Version 8.3(1)

Prior to software version 8.3(1), instead of configuring a network object group, the nat and global statements were used to configure port address translation.

Use the command *show* version to display the software version running on your ASA. If your ASA is running a version earlier than 8.3(1), use the following commands to configure port address translation.

nat

The *nat* command enables network address translation on the specified interface for the specified subnet.

In this sample, configuration, NAT is enabled on the inside interface for hosts on the 192.168.1.0/24 subnet. The number "1" is the NAT I.D. which will be used by the *global* command to associate a global address or pool with the inside addresses. (Note: NAT 0 is used to prevent the specified group of addresses from being translated.)

```
ciscoasa(config)# nat (inside) 1 192.168.1.0 255.255.255.0
```

global

The *global* command works in tandem with the nat command. It identifies the interface (usually outside) through which traffic from nat'ed hosts (usually inside hosts) must flow. It also identifies the global address which nat'ed hosts will use to connect to the outside world.

In the following sample, the hosts associated with NAT I.D. 1 will use the global address 12.3.4.5 on the outside interface.

```
ciscoasa(config)# global (outside) 1 12.3.4.5
```

In the following sample, the interface statement tells the firewall that hosts associated with NAT I.D. 1 will use the DHCP-assigned global address on the outside interface.

```
ciscoasa(config)# global (outside) 1 interface
```

Hands-On Exercise 1.4:
Using the Eight Commands Required to Enable Basic Firewall Functionality

In this exercise, you will use the command-line interface to build a basic firewall configuration that will allow local traffic out, but not allow external traffic in.

Watch the Video

There is a video on my YouTube channel in which I demonstrate the following procedures. Watch the video at http://youtu.be/Y0ZnRmgINgE.

Exercise Diagram

For this exercise, you will connect your management workstation to the ASA security appliance using the serial console cable and an Ethernet cable. It is also necessary to connect the outside interface to the public Internet using an Ethernet cable.

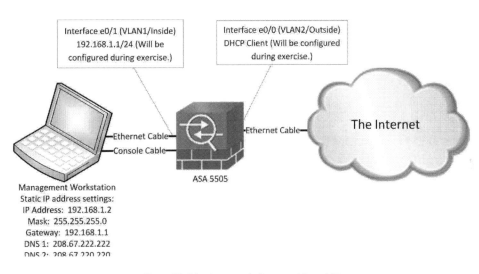

Figure 23: A basic network diagram with an ASA

Exercise Prerequisites

This exercise requires that you have an ASA, a Cisco console cable, Internet access, and a computer with terminal emulation software such as PuTTY.

Exercise Steps

Assign Interface Names, IP Addresses, and a Default Route

1. Log in with a blank username and password.

   ```
   ciscoasa> en
   Password: <Enter>
   ```

2. Identify the logical (VLAN) interfaces, assign names and security levels to them:

   ```
   ciscoasa# conf t
   ```

   (The ASA will now ask if you wish to enable anonymous reporting. Enter **N** for no.)

   ```
   ciscoasa(config)# interface vlan1
   ciscoasa(config-if)# nameif inside
   INFO: Security level for "inside" set to 100 by default.
   ciscoasa(config-if)# interface vlan2
   ciscoasa(config-if)# nameif outside
   INFO: Security level for "outside" set to 0 by default
   ```

3. Assign physical interfaces to each of the logical interfaces and enable the physical interfaces:

   ```
   ciscoasa(config-if)# interface ethernet 0/0
   ciscoasa(config-if)# switchport access vlan 2
   ciscoasa(config-if)# no shutdown
   ciscoasa(config-if)# interface ethernet 0/1
   ciscoasa(config-if)# switchport access vlan 1
   ciscoasa(config-if)# no shutdown
   ```

```
                                                        COM5 - PuTTY
Type help or '?' for a list of available commands.
ciscoasa> en
Password:
ciscoasa# conf t
ciscoasa(config)#

***************************** NOTICE ****************************

Help to improve the ASA platform by enabling anonymous reporting,
which allows Cisco to securely receive minimal error and health
information from the device. To learn more about this feature,
please visit: http://www.cisco.com/go/smartcall

Would you like to enable anonymous error reporting to help improve
the product? [Y]es, [N]o, [A]sk later: n

In the future, if you would like to enable this feature,
issue the command "call-home reporting anonymous".

Please remember to save your configuration.

ciscoasa(config)# interface vlan1
ciscoasa(config-if)# nameif inside
INFO: Security level for "inside" set to 100 by default.
ciscoasa(config-if)# interface vlan2
ciscoasa(config-if)# nameif outside
INFO: Security level for "outside" set to 0 by default.
ciscoasa(config-if)# interface ethernet 0/0
ciscoasa(config-if)# switchport access vlan 2
ciscoasa(config-if)# no shutdown
ciscoasa(config-if)# interface ethernet 0/1
ciscoasa(config-if)# switchport access vlan 1
ciscoasa(config-if)# no shutdown
ciscoasa(config-if)#
```

Figure 24: Starting the basic configuration

4. Assign IP addresses to the logical interfaces. Use a static address on the inside interface and a DHCP assigned address on the outside interface:

ciscoasa(config-if)# **interface vlan 2**

ciscoasa(config-if)# **ip address dhcp setroute**

ciscoasa(config-if)# **interface vlan 1**

ciscoasa(config-if)# **ip address 192.168.1.1**

```
ciscoasa(config-if)#
ciscoasa(config-if)# interface vlan 2
ciscoasa(config-if)# ip address dhcp setroute
ciscoasa(config-if)# interface vlan 2
ciscoasa(config-if)# ip address 192.168.1.1
ciscoasa(config-if)# _
```

Figure 25:
Configuring IP addresses
on the interfaces

If your ASA's outside interface uses a static IP address and default gateway supplied by a service provider, perform the following steps, otherwise skip to step 7:

5. Configure the address on the outside interface:

   ```
   ciscoasa(config-if)# interface vlan 2
   ```

   ciscoasa(config-if)# **ip address w.x.y.z a.b.c.d** (where w.x.y.z is the outside address supplied by your service provider and a.b.c.d is the subnet mask supplied by your service provider)

6. Configure a default route:

   ciscoasa(config-if)# **route outside 0 0 w.x.y.z** (where w.x.y.z is the address of the default gateway supplied to you by your service provider)

Configure Port Address Translation

7. Create a network object group to identify the IP addresses of hosts permitted to use PAT. In this example, it will be all hosts:

   ```
   ciscoasa# conf t
   ```

   ```
   ciscoasa(config)# object network obj _ any
   ```

   ```
   ciscoasa(config-network-object)# subnet 0.0.0.0 0.0.0.0
   ```

   ```
   ciscoasa(config-network-object)# nat (inside,outside) dynamic interface
   ```

```
ciscoasa# conf t
ciscoasa(config)# object network obj_any
ciscoasa(config-network-object)# subnet 0.0.0.0 0.0.0.0
ciscoasa(config-network-object)# nat (inside,outside) dynamic interface
ciscoasa(config-network-object)#
```

Figure 26: Configuring Port Address Translation (PAT)

If the ASA Doesn't Accept the Port Address Translation Commands

If step seven doesn't work, the most likely reason is because your ASA is loaded with a software version prior to 8.3. This can happen even on a brand new ASA. Check the software version with the command *show version*. If your software is earlier than 8.3, say 8.2(5) for example, you can either upgrade to a more recent version or see the instructions earlier in this chapter. This book is based on software version 9.0(4) and 9.2(2)4.

Test the Configuration

8. Assign a static IP address to your management workstation to test your configuration (the following steps are for computers running the Windows 7 operating system):

   a. Click on Start, then click on Control Panel

   b. Click on *Network and Internet Connections*

   c. Click on *Network and Sharing Center*

   d. Click on *Change Adapter Settings*

   e. Right-click on *Local Area Connection* for the wired connection and select *Properties*

   f. Scroll down to and double-click on *Internet Protocol Version 4 (TCP/IPv4)* to display its properties sheet

   g. Select the radio button labeled Use the following IP address and enter the following parameters:

      i. IP address: 192.168.1.2

      ii. Subnet mask: 255.255.255.0

      iii. Default gateway: 192.168.1.1

      iv. DNS server: 208.67.222.222 and 208.67.220.220 (these are Open DNS's public DNS servers)

   h. Click OK as needed to save the configuration and exit the applet.

9. Test your configuration by attempting to connect to a public website from your PC such as http://www.soundtraining.net.

10. When you have successfully connected to the website, restore your computer's IP configuration to obtain an IP address automatically.

Adaptive Security Device Manager

The Adaptive Security Device Manager (ASDM) is the Java-based GUI tool for managing Cisco ASA Security Appliances.

With the Java plugin, it is often not a matter of having the most recent version, but having a *supported* version. If you have problems running ASDM, even small, seemingly unrelated problems, ensure that you are running a supported version of Java for your ASDM version.

The version of Java required varies based on the version of the ASDM. You can check the required Java version for your version of ASDM by reviewing the release notes on the Cisco website for the particular version of ASDM which you're running. Use the command *show version* on the ASA to determine which version of ASDM you're running. Then, use this search string to find the release notes for your version of ASDM: *site:cisco.com asdm release notes*.

A separate demo program is available that simulates many functions of the ASA in the ASDM without requiring a physical security appliance. You can download the demo program from http://www.cisco.com/cisco/web/download/index.html. (A Cisco support contract is required for most downloads.)

The ASDM includes several wizards to assist in tasks such as building an initial configuration, setting up VPNs, configuring high availability and scalability, configuring unified communications, and traffic analysis with the packet capture wizard.

Hands-On Exercise 1.5:
Removing the Existing Configuration on Your Security Appliance and Installing the Factory Default Configuration

In this exercise, you will once again return your ASA to the basic factory default configuration.

Exercise Diagram
This exercise uses the same diagram as the previous exercise.

Exercise Prerequisites
The prerequisites for this exercise are the same as for the previous exercise.

Exercise Steps
1. Log in to the console port on your ASA and enter privileged mode:

   ```
   ciscoasa> en
   Password: <Enter>
   ciscoasa#
   ```

2. Enter configuration mode:

   ```
   ciscoasa# config t
   ciscoasa(config)#
   ```

3. Enter the following commands to reset your ASA to factory defaults (if your appliance asks to save the configuration, say "no"):

   ```
   ciscoasa(config)# write erase
   Erase configuration in flash memory? [confirm]<Enter>
   ciscoasa(config)# reload
   Proceed with reload? [confirm]<Enter>
   ```

   (If your security appliance asks if you want to save the modified configuration, say "no".)

4. When your ASA finishes reloading, it will ask if you want to pre-configure the firewall through interactive prompts. Type no and press the Enter key.

5. Set your ASA to its factory default configuration with the following commands (in configuration mode):

```
ciscoasa> enable
Password: <Enter>
ciscoasa#
ciscoasa# conf t
```

(Again, the ASA will ask if you wish to enable anonymous reporting. Enter **N** for no.)

```
ciscoasa(config)# config factory-default
```

(Press the space bar at each "—more—" prompt.)

6. Reset your management workstation to obtain an IP address automatically:

    a. Click on *Start*, then click on *Control Panel*

    b. Click on *Network and Internet Connections*

    c. Click on *Network Connections*

    d. Right-click on *Local Area Connection* and select *Properties*

    e. Scroll down to and double-click on *Internet Protocol (TCP/IP)* to display its properties sheet

    f. Select the radio button labeled *Obtain an IP address automatically*.

    g. Click OK as needed to save the configuration and exit the applet.

    h. Confirm that your PC obtained an IP address by clicking *Start*, then *Run*. (Alternatively, you can use the key combination of Win+R.) In the Run dialog box, type *cmd* and press the Enter key.

    i. In the Command Line Interface window that appears, type *ipconfig* and press the Enter key.

    j. You should see an IP address of 192.168.1.5 (or possibly a different number in the fourth position) with a subnet mask of 255.255.255.0 and a default gateway of 192.168.1.1. If you do not see these values, type the command *ipconfig /renew* in the Command Line Interface window and press the Enter key. You should now see an IP address of 192.168.1.5 (or possibly a slightly different number in the fourth position) with a subnet mask of 255.255.255.0 and a default gateway of 192.168.1.1. If you do not see these values, review the preceding steps and, if necessary, repeat them.

Hands-On Exercise 1.6:
Using ASDM to Build an Initial Configuration on Your ASA

In this portion of the exercise, you will use the Adaptive Security Device Manager to build an initial (basic) configuration on your security appliance. This configuration will be the basis for all subsequent exercises.

Exercise Prerequisites

This exercise is based on ASA software version 9.2(2)4 and ASDM version 7.3(1)101. If your software and ASDM versions are different, you may encounter different commands or the screen captures may look slightly different. As long as your ASA software version is at least 8.3, most of the commands should still work. Some may require slight adjustments. This exercise requires that you have completed exercise 1.5.

Exercise Diagram

For this exercise, you will connect your management workstation to the ASA security appliance using the serial console cable and an Ethernet cable. It is also necessary to connect the outside interface to the public Internet using an Ethernet cable.

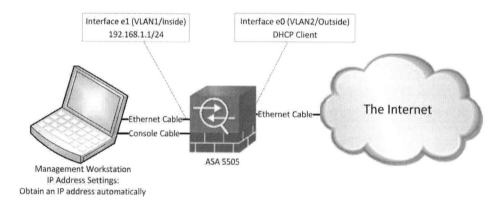

Figure 27: A basic network diagram with an ASA and a single computer

Exercise Steps

From your PC, use the browser to connect to the ASA:

1. On your PC, click Start>Run (or use the key combination of Win+R)

2. Enter the following URL in the Run dialog window:

   https://192.168.1.1

   (note the use of the "s" in the protocol type)

3. For the purpose of this exercise, ignore the certificate warning and proceed to the website. (Obviously, in a real-world environment, you would use standard security precautions before proceeding.)

4. If you get an ActiveX/Java warning in your browser, run the add-in.

5. After several seconds, the Cisco ASDM 7.1(2) page should appear. If it appears, go to step 7. If, instead, you see a pop-up error saying "Unable to launch device manager", you probably need to adjust the Java security settings on your computer.

Figure 28:
An ASDM warning

6. To deal with this error, go to Control Panel >> Java. Select the Security tab and add the IP address of the ASA to the Java Exception Site List. (When you add the ASA's IP address, you must also include https://.)

Figure 29:
Creating a Java exception in
the Java control panel

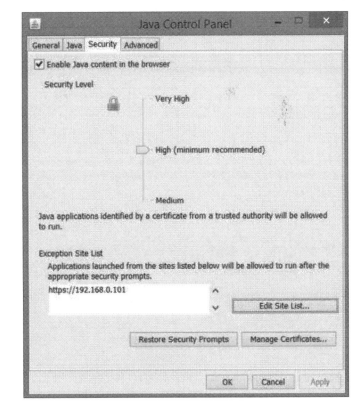

7. If a button is visible in the lower right-hand corner of the screen labeled *Run Startup Wizard*, proceed to step 11. Otherwise, proceed to step 8.

8. If a button is visible at the bottom of the screen prompting you to install Java, you must install the Java runtime environment. Simply click it to install Java.

9. Java will take some time to install and may appear to stall. It will, however, eventually complete the installation.

10. When Java Runtime is completed, you can continue the exercise by refreshing your browser.

11. Click the button in the lower right-hand corner of the screen labeled *Run Startup Wizard*. You will receive several security warnings and additional requests for authentication. Different browsers have different ways of dealing with Java. You might also have to tell your browser to keep a file named startup.jnlp and then click on the downloaded file to run it. Click Yes or OK on all subsequent security warnings.

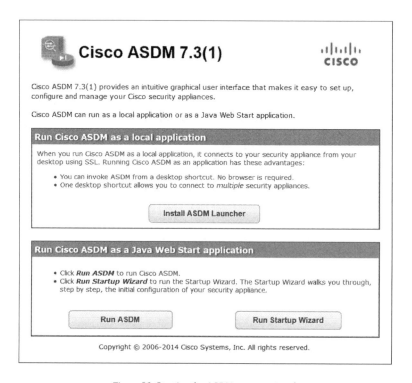

Figure 30: Starting the ASDM startup wizard

12. Depending on the browser you're using, you may get prompted to run Java or to allow Java applications to run. You must say yes when prompted in order to use the ASDM.

13. You'll be prompted to authenticate, but since no usernames and passwords have been configured, leave both fields empty and click the button labeled OK.

Figure 31:
The initial authentication request.

14. If a Windows security alert appears, click the button labeled *"Unblock"* or *"Allow"*.

15. A Cisco Smart Call Home window will appear. Select the radio button labeled *Do not enable Smart Call Home* and press OK.

16. Press OK again to confirm that you do not want to enable Smart Call Home (You'd think it would have believed you the first time! Jeezsh.).

17. The *Startup Wizard: Starting Point* window will appear. Ensure that the radio button for *Modify existing configuration* is selected and click the button at the bottom of the window labeled Next.

18. The *Startup Wizard: Basic Configuration* window will appear.

19. Enter the *ASA Host Name* for your security appliance. For the purpose of this exercise, you can just call it *asa01*. Feel free to get more creative if you're really inspired.

20. Enter *soundtraining.local* for the domain name. (You can enter any domain you want. I use *soundtraining.local* since my company's name is soundtraining.net and I'm pretty shameless about promoting it.)

21. Check the box labeled *Change the privileged mode (enable) password*. Leave the Old Password field blank and enter *p@ss5678* for the New Password and confirm it.

22. Click the button labeled *Next*.

23. The *Interface Selection* window appears. Configure the settings on this page as follows:

    a. Outside VLAN: Leave the default settings in place (VLAN 2, enable VLAN)

    b. Inside VLAN: Leave the default settings in place (VLAN 1, enable VLAN)

    c. Older versions of the ASDM will include a DMZ VLAN option: If you have that option, choose *Do not configure* and clear the check box labeled Enable VLAN.

24. Click the button labeled *Next*.

25. The *Switch Port Allocation* page appears. Although it is not necessary to make any changes on this page, notice that ports Ethernet 0/1 through Ethernet 0/7 are allocated to VLAN 1 (the inside VLAN) and port Ethernet 0/0 is allocated to VLAN 2 (the outside VLAN). Click the button labeled *Next*.

26. The *Interface IP Address Configuration* page appears.

    a. In the *Outside IP Address* section, choose the default setting to use DHCP.) Also, be sure to check the box labeled *Obtain default route using DHCP*.

    b. In the *Inside IP Address* section, leave the default settings in place (192.168.1.1 and 255.255.255.0)

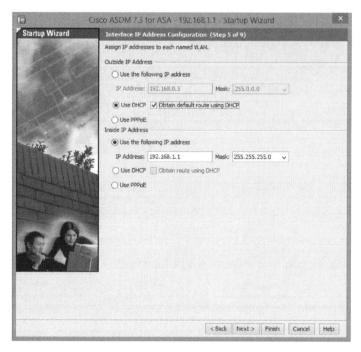

Figure 32:
Interface IP Address Configuration

27. Click the button labeled *Next >*.

28. The *DHCP Server* page appears.

29. Ensure that the checkbox to *Enable DHCP server on the inside interface* is selected.

30. In the *DHCP Address Pool* section, accept the default starting and ending IP addresses (this is based on the licensed number of users).

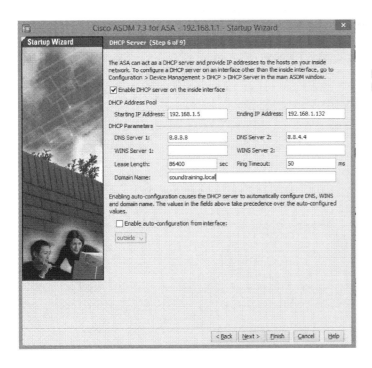

Figure 33:
DHCP Server setup

31. In the *DHCP Parameters* section, enter the following parameters:

    a. DNS Server 1: 8.8.8.8 (A Google public DNS server)

    b. DNS Server 2: 8.8.4.4 (Also a Google public DNS server)

    c. WINS Server 1: blank

    d. WINS Server 2: blank

    e. Lease Length: 86400 secs (default is 3600 seconds; 86400 secs is one day)

    f. Ping Timeout: 50 ms (default is 50 ms)

    g. Domain name: soundtraining. local (you can change this to whatever you want)

32. Click the button labeled *Next >*.

33. The *Address Translation (NAT/PAT)* page appears. Select the radio button labeled *Use Port Address Translation (PAT)* and ensure that the button labeled *Use the IP address on the outside interface* is selected.

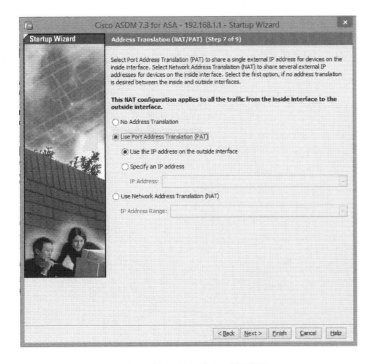

Figure 34: Address Translation (NAT/PAT)

51

34. Click the button labeled *Next >*.

35. The *Administrative Access* page appears. The default settings allow access from the 192.168.1.0 network (which is what has enabled you to run the ASDM up to this point). It is not necessary to make any changes. (You can also enable SSH and Telnet access on this page, but you will do that manually later in the book.)

36. Click the button labeled *Next >*.

37. The *Startup Wizard Summary* page appears. Review the settings to ensure they're what you expect. When you are satisfied, click the button labeled *Finish*.

38. The device will prompt you for a username and password. Leave the username field blank and enter *p@ss5678* for the password.

39. You are now logged in to the Adaptive Security Device Manager.

What is Smart Call Home?

After building the configuration, the ASDM may ask you if you want to enable *Smart Call Home*. This is a feature which was introduced into the ASA firewalls in software version 8.2. *Smart Call Home* allows for periodic monitoring of the firewall device. It provides real-time troubleshooting information to the Cisco Technical Assistance Center. *Smart Call Home* is included in a Cisco SmartNET contract. For the purpose of this exercise, do not enable *Smart Call Home*. For more information about its capabilities, see the video at http://www.cisco.com/warp/public/437/services/smartcallhome/.

Hands-On Exercise 1.7: Previewing Commands

Configure the ASDM to allow you to preview the commands you enable before sending them to the device with the following commands:

1. In the menu bar at the top of the ASDM window, click on *Tools*, then click on *Preferences* …

2. In the *Preferences* window, under the *General* tab, check the box to *Preview commands before sending them to the device.* and click *OK*.

CHAPTER 2:
Backing Up and Restoring Configurations and Software Images

"What boots up must come down. "

—Unknown

Analyzing the Base Configuration of the Security Appliance

The Cisco Adaptive Security Appliance ships with a default configuration that allows rapid deployment in a basic firewall mode. Out of the box, the ASA provides DHCP services to allow internal clients to auto-configure their TCP/IP settings. Additionally, the ASA provides Port Address Translation (PAT) service.

In the following exercise, you will use CLI commands to observe and record basic information about your appliance. You will also use PuTTY's logging facility to save the information to a text file.

Saving Your ASA's Base Configuration

It is a good idea to record important information about your ASA for future reference including the license information and activation key. In the following exercises, you will review your appliance's hardware and software configuration including license, serial number, and activation key and create a text file backup of the information.

Hands-On Exercise 2.1:
Confirm Network Connectivity

Exercise Diagram

For this exercise, you will use a similar network configuration to that used in chapter one. Unlike the start of chapter one, you must configure your management workstation to obtain an IP address automatically from the DHCP server running on the security appliance. If you're simply continuing from the last exercise (1.6), your computer should already be configured correctly for this exercise. You will connect your management workstation to the ASA security appliance using both the serial console cable and an Ethernet cable. It is also necessary to connect the outside interface to the public Internet using an Ethernet cable.

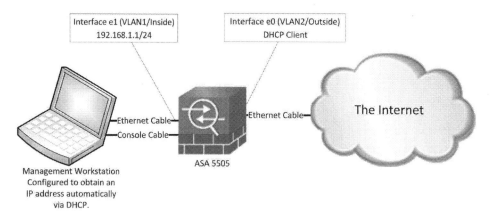

Figure 35: Basic network diagram with ASA using DHCP

Exercise Prerequisites

This exercise has the same prerequisites as the previous exercise.

Exercise Steps

In its default configuration, the ASA will provide DHCP services. Test the DHCP service on your PC with the following commands:

1. Click Start>Run (or use the key combination of Win+R)

2. Type **cmd**

3. In the command prompt window, enter **ipconfig /renew**.

4. After a few seconds, issue the command ipconfig and you should see IP address parameters similar to this:

```
Connection-specific DNS Suffix  . :
Link-local IPv6 Address . . . . . : fe80::3440:6550:e8f:2b05%3
IPv4 Address. . . . . . . . . . . : 192.168.1.5
Subnet Mask . . . . . . . . . . . : 255.255.255.0
Default Gateway . . . . . . . . . : 192.168.1.1
```

Figure 36:
Viewing a computer's
IP address

If your settings are substantially different from this, review the preceding steps and make corrections as needed.

5. Confirm connectivity by pinging your ASA's inside interface from your PC, using the following command:

C:\>**ping 192.168.1.1**

6. You should get four replies back from the ASA. If not, check cables and connections, then repeat the previous steps.

Hands-On Exercise 2.2:
Review and Backup Configuration Information

Exercise Prerequisites

This exercise requires you to have a folder on your management workstation in the root of your C drive named *myconfigs*.

Exercise Diagram

This exercise uses the same diagram as the previous exercise.

Exercise Steps

1. Create a folder on your management workstation to store all of your configuration files: On your management workstation, create a folder called c:\myconfigs (alternatively, you could create a folder on a flash drive to store all of your configuration files).

2. Using PuTTY to connect to your computer's serial port, in your ASA's command-line interface (CLI), enter the following commands:

ciscoasa> **enable**

Password:<Enter>

ciscoasa# **terminal pager 0**

(Terminal pager determines how many lines of text will be shown on your monitor in a single page. Setting terminal pager to 0 disables paging.)

3. Open the PuTTY configuration menu by clicking on the small PuTTY icon in the upper left-hand corner of the PuTTY window.

4. Click on the menu option *Change Settings..*

5. In the PuTTY Reconfiguration window, in the category tree on the left, under *Session*, click on *Logging*.

6. On the right-hand side of the *Reconfiguration* window, under *Session logging*, click the radio button labeled *Printable output*.

7. In the Log file name field, browse to *c:\myconfigs*. Name the file asainfo.txt and click *Save*.

8. Click *Apply*.

9. In your ASA's console window, enter the following command:
   ciscoasa# **show version**

10. When the output finishes displaying, restore the paging of command-line output with the following command:
    ciscoasa# **terminal pager 24**

11. Click again on the PuTTY icon in the upper right-hand corner of the PuTTY window, click again on *Change Settings …*

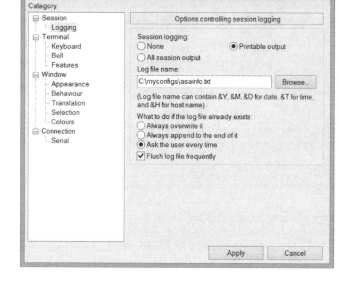

Figure 37:
Configuring PuTTY for logging

12. On the right-hand side of the PuTTY *Reconfiguration* window, under *Session logging*, click the radio button labeled *None* to disable logging.

13. Click *Apply*.

14. Find the folder *c:\myconfigs* (or whatever folder you created to store your configuration files), then find the file asainfo.txt. Double-click on it to open it and view the contents. If your PC displays a single text-heavy paragraph instead of a nicely formatted configuration file, right-click on asainfo.txt with your mouse, choose *"Open with Wordpad"* to view the contents.

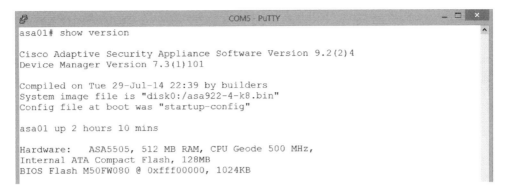

Figure 38: The top of the output of the show version command.

15. What is the system image file and where is it stored?

    (The system image file will have a name similar to asa922-4-k8.bin and should be located in flash, also known as disk0.)

16. How long has the ASA been up? This ASA has been up for 2 hours and 10 minutes.

17. Just under the uptime information you'll find hardware information. How much RAM is available on the ASA? My ASA 5505 has 512MB of RAM.

18. What type of CPU does the ASA 5505 use? (ASA 5505 appliances use a Geode processor which is often found in purpose-built devices such as the ASA. Depending on the type of ASA you have, you could see processors such as a Pentium II, a Pentium 4 Celeron, or others.)

19. How much Flash Memory is available on the ASA? The ASA in the screen capture has 128MB of compact flash.

for

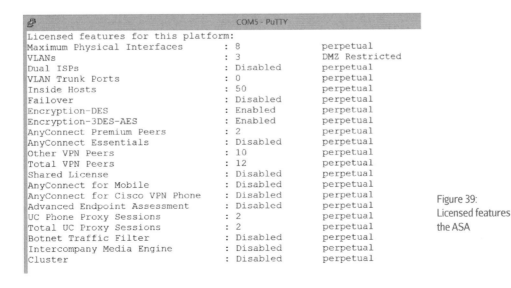

Figure 39:
Licensed features
the ASA

20. Scroll farther down through the file to the licensed features section. How many physical interfaces are supported on this ASA? This ASA has eight physical interfaces.

21. How many VLANs does this ASA support? The number of supported VLANs will vary based on the license. A 5505 with a base license, such as the one used in the screen capture supports three VLANs, but one of them is restricted.

22. How many inside hosts are supported with this license? The number varies based on the license. This ASA supports 50 inside hosts.

23. How many AnyConnect Premium Peers are supported with this license? Two.

24. How about other VPN peers? 10. (As with the number of inside hosts, this number also varies based on the license.)

```
This platform has a Base license.

Serial Number: ▉▉▉▉▉▉▉▉
Running Permanent Activation Key: ▉▉▉▉▉▉▉ ▉▉▉▉▉▉▉ ▉▉▉▉▉▉▉ ▉▉▉▉▉▉▉ ▉▉
▉▉▉▉▉▉
Configuration register is 0x1
Configuration last modified by enable_15 at 19:39:28.349 UTC Wed Dec 24 2014
asa01#
```

Figure 40: License information

25. Scroll to very bottom of the file. What type of license is associated with this ASA? This ASA has a Base license.

26. What is the serial number of this ASA? (The serial number is important to note when you need to obtain service from Cisco and when you want to upgrade your device's license.)

27. Notice the activation key. The activation key is tied to your device's serial number and determines the features that are enabled on your device.

28. What is the configuration register for this ASA? This ASA's configuration register is 0x1, the default. The configuration register is a 16-bit software value that tells the device how to boot. For example, in a previous exercise, you modified the configuration register to 0x41 which told the device to ignore its saved configuration, thus allowing you to perform password recovery procedures on the device.

Backing Up Your Configuration and Your Software

Now that you have built a base configuration on your firewall, you will want to create a backup to facilitate disaster recovery. In the following exercises, you will backup and restore your security appliance's running configuration to and from a TFTP server.

The process of backing up your ASA involves backing up your configuration file and the device's software image. Both are stored in flash memory. The configuration file is called startup-config. The software image has a filename similar to asa904-k8.bin. You should also backup the device's ASDM image which has a filename similar to asdm-731.bin.

Hands-On Exercise 2.3:
Install and Configure the TFTP Server Software on Your PC

Exercise Diagram

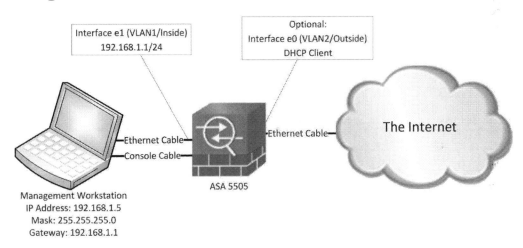

Figure 41: Network diagram preparing for a TFTP server

Exercise Prerequisites

- A management workstation computer, connected to the ASA via both Ethernet and serial console cable

- TFTP server software installed on the management workstation. The exercise is written using TFTPD32, but any TFTP server software should work

Exercise Steps

1. On an Internet-connected PC, navigate to http://tftpd32.jounin.net/ and download tftpd32 or tftpd64, depending on your PC's processor architecture.

2. After you download the TFTP server, install it on your management workstation.

3. When the installation completes, click on Start>All Programs or, on Windows 8/8.1, click on the start button, then find tftpd. Start it.

4. In the TFTP server application window, notice that the current directory is c:\Program Files (x86)\tftpd32 or something similar.

5. Change the TFTP root folder to c:\myconfigs (or whatever folder you created earlier to store your configurations).

6. If you have multiple interfaces configured on your management workstation, you will also have to select the server interface by using the Server interface pulldown just below the current directory.

It may also be necessary to configure the Windows firewall to allow incoming TFTP connections by clicking the button labeled Unblock, if prompted. If you need to manually configure the port number on your firewall, TFTP operates on UDP port 69.

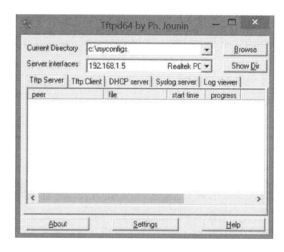

Figure 42:
Configuring Tftpd

Hands-On Exercise 2.4:
The Cisco ASA Configuration Backup Process

Exercise Diagram

The exercise diagram is the same as used in the previous exercise.

Exercise Prerequisites

The prerequisites are the same as used in the previous exercise.

Exercise Steps

In your security appliance's CLI, execute the following commands to back up your running configuration to a TFTP server.

1. `ciscoasa>` **`enable`** `<Enter>`

   `ciscoasa#` **`copy running-config tftp://192.168.1.5`** `<Enter>`
   (where 192.168.1.5 is the address of your management workstation. If yours' is different, make necessary adjustments.)

   `Source filename [running-config]?` `<Enter>`

   `Address or name of remote host [192.168.1.5]?` `<Enter>`
   (where 192.168.1.5 is the IP address of your management workstation)

   `Destination filename [running-config]?` **`asa _ backup.txt`** `<Enter>`

2. You will see a confirmation of the transfer in the appliance's console output.

3. Confirm the transfer by checking for the file in the TFTP root folder.

Hands-On Exercise 2.5:
The Cisco ASA Configuration Restore Process

In this exercise, you will make a minor change in the device's current configuration. You will then restore the backed up configuration from the previous exercise. If you do the following steps correctly, you will see the minor change erased as the previous configuration is restored.

Exercise Diagram

The exercise diagram is the same as used in the previous exercise.

Prerequisites

The prerequisites are the same as used in the previous exercise.

Exercise Steps

Rename your security appliance with the following commands:

1. `ciscoasa#` **`config t`** `<enter>`
   `ciscoasa(config)#` **`hostname asatest`** `<enter>`
   `asatest(config)#` **`exit`** `<enter>`
   `asatest#`

Notice that the security appliance's prompt has changed to reflect the new hostname. You will now copy the previously backed up configuration from the TFTP server to the security appliance's running configuration with the following commands:

2. `asatest#` **`copy tftp://192.168.1.5/asa _ backup.txt`** `running-config <Enter>`

   (192.168.1.5 is the IP address of your management workstation. If yours' is different, you must adjust settings or commands accordingly.)

3. `Address or name of remote host [192.168.1.5]?<Enter>`

   (where 192.168.1.5 is the address of your management workstation)

4. `Source filename [asa _ backup.txt]? <enter>`

5. `Destination filename [running-config]?<Enter>`

You will notice confirmation of the transfer, plus some error messages related to duplicate NAT entries. When the transfer is completed, notice that your security appliance's prompt reflects the original hostname.

Backing Up, Upgrading, and Restoring the Software Image

In the following series of exercises, you will create backups of your ASA's software using a TFTP server. You will then perform an upgrade of the ASA's software image using several different techniques. Additionally, you will copy the ASA software from your TFTP server into the ASA's flash memory using the same techniques you would use to restore a backup of the software or to perform an upgrade.

Hands-On Exercise 2.6:
Backup Your ASA's Software to the TFTP Server

Exercise Diagram

The exercise diagram is the same as used in the previous exercise.

Exercise Prerequisites

The prerequisites are the same as used in the previous exercise.

Exercise Steps

Ensure that the TFTP server is running on your management workstation.

1. Display the contents of your security appliance's flash memory:

   `ciscoasa#` **`show flash`** `<enter>`

   Notice a file named similarly to asa922-4-k8.bin. That is the security appliance's software image (similar to a computer's operating system).

2. Copy the software image to your TFTP server with the following commands:

   ```
   ciscoasa# copy flash tftp <enter>
   ```

   ```
   Source filename []:asa922-4-k8.bin <enter>
   ```

   (Note: If your security appliance is running a different version of the software, you will have to adjust these commands to reflect the correct version numbers.)

   ```
   Address or name of remote host []? 192.168.1.5 <enter>
   ```

   (where 192.168.1.5 is the address of your management workstation)

   ```
   Destination filename [asa911-k8.bin]? <Enter>
   ```

3. Your security appliance console output will display many lines of exclamation marks as it copies the software to the TFTP server. This process can take several minutes. You can watch the progress in the TFTP server console window. (This is also a good time to take a short break.)

In a real-world setting, you will probably want to back up the ASDM image as well. It has a filename similar to *asdm-731-101.bin*. The procedures for backing up the ASDM image are identical to those above, except that you must change the name in step two from the ASA software image filename to the ASDM image filename.

Upgrading the ASA Software Image

As with all computer software, upgraded versions of the ASA software are frequently made available by Cisco. The decision to upgrade is usually based on the desire to address security vulnerabilities or to take advantage of new capabilities. Prior to performing an upgrade to your ASA's software image, review the release notes for the new version you're considering, paying particular attention to any new memory or other hardware requirements. Familiarize yourself with any command syntax changes. When you make the decision to proceed, before actually performing the upgrade, test the entire process in a lab environment, and, of course, backup your existing system including configuration files. Plan on performing the upgrade during a slow time, such as overnight on a weekend, just in case of problems.

You can upgrade using either the command line or the ASDM. In the next exercises, you'll use both techniques to perform the upgrade.

Hands-On Exercise 2.7:
Upgrading the ASA Software in the Command Line Environment

In this exercise, you will upgrade the ASA software image in the command line environment using a TFTP server.

Exercise Diagram

The exercise diagram is the same as used in the previous exercise.

Exercise Prerequisites

- In addition to the prerequisites for the previous exercise, this exercise requires that you have access to an upgraded version of the Cisco ASA software. You can download the latest version from cisco. com, if you have a SMARTnet support contract.

- A copy of the software image must be located in the TFTP server's root directory, in my case c:\myconfigs.

- You must also ensure that your ASA meets the minimum hardware requirements for the software version you choose to download and install. Visit http://www.cisco.com/c/en/us/td/docs/ security/asa/compatibility/asamatrx.html to check for compatibility.

Exercise Steps

1. Use the command *show flash* to review the contents of your ASA's flash memory to ensure there's enough room in flash for the new software image. If not, you will need to free up space in flash before performing the upgrade. Use the command *del disk0:* with the filename to be deleted. As you can see in the following screen capture, there is a total of 43216896 bytes of free memory. The software image to which I will upgrade is 29,754 KB in size, so the upgrade should work.

```
ciscoasa#
ciscoasa# show flash
--#--  --length--  -----date/time------  path
  10   4096        Jul 29 2007 19:52:06  log
  18   4096        Jul 13 2010 11:02:44  coredumpinfo
  19   59          Mar 15 2011 14:44:34  coredumpinfo/coredump.cfg
  98   27629568    Sep 05 2014 20:17:42  asa904-k8.bin
  99   35634248    Nov 22 2014 01:21:24  anyconnect-win-3.1.05187-k9.pkg
 101   340         Nov 22 2014 14:40:04  RemoteUsers_client_profile.xml
  17   4096        Jul 29 2007 19:52:24  crypto_archive
 102   19884888    Nov 21 2014 05:49:26  asdm-731-101.bin

127111168 bytes total (43216896 bytes free)
ciscoasa#
```

Figure 43:
Viewing the contents
of flash memory

2. On the TFTP server, ensure the current directory is set to your desired directory, in my case c:\myconfigs. (You can use the Browse button to set the directory.)

3. Click the *Show Dir* button to list the contents of the current directory.

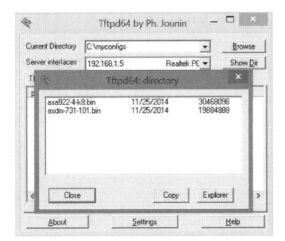

Figure 44:
Viewing the contents of
the TFTP root directory

4. Use your mouse to select the software image filename, in this case, asa922-4-k8.bin. In PuTTY, when you select text with your mouse, it is automatically copied to the clipboard. You can then simply right-click to paste the copied text into the terminal window at the position of the cursor. Try it on the next command. Type the command up through the last forward slash, then right-click with your mouse to paste the selected text.

5. Use the following command to copy the software image from the TFTP server to the ASA:

    ```
    copy tftp://192.168.1.5/asa922-4-k8.bin flash
    ```

6. The copy process may take a while.

```
ciscoasa#
ciscoasa# copy tftp://192.168.1.5/asa922-4-k8.bin flash

Address or name of remote host [192.168.1.5]?

Source filename [asa922-4-k8.bin]?

Destination filename [asa922-4-k8.bin]?

Accessing tftp://192.168.1.5/asa922-4-k8.bin...!!!!!!!!!!!!!!!!!!!!!!!!!!!!!!!!!!!!!!!!!!!!!!!!!!!!!!!!!!!!!!!!!!!!!!!!!!!
!!!!!!!!!!!!!!!!!!!!!!!!!!!!!!!!!!!!!!!!!!!!!!!!!!!!!!!!!!!!!!!!!!!!!!!!!!!!!!!!!!!!!!!!!!!!!!!!!!!!!!!!!!!!!!!!!!!!!!
!!!!!!!!!!!!!!!!!!!!!!!!!!!!!!!!!!!!!!!!!!!!!!!!!!!!!!!!!!!!!!!!!!!!!!!!!!!!!!!!!!!!!!!!!!!!!!!!!!!!!!!!!!!!!!!!!!!!!!
!!!!!!!!!!!!!!!!!!!!!!!!!!!!!!!!!!!!!!!!!!!!!!!!!!!!!!!!!!!!!!!!!!!!!!!!!!!!!!!!!!!!!!!!!!!!!!!!!!!!!!!!!!!!!!!!!!!!!!
!!!!!!!!!!!!!!!!!!!!!!!!!!!!!!!!!!!!!!!!!!!!!!!!!!!!!!!!!!!!!!!!!!!!!!!!!!!!!!!!!!!!!!!!!!!!!!!!!!!!!!!!!!!!!!!!!!!!!!
!!!!!!!!!!!!!!!!!!!!!!!!!!!!!!!!!!!!!!!!!!!!!!!!!!!!!!!!!!!!!!!!!!!!!!!!!!!!!!!!!!!!!!!!!!!!!!!!!!!!!!!!!!!!!!!!!!!!!!
!!!!!!!!!!!!!!!!!!!!!!!!!!!!!!!!!!!!!!!!!!!!!!!!!!!!!!!!!!!!!!!!!!!!!!!!!!!!!!!
```

Figure 45: Upgrading the ASA software image in the CLI

7. When it completes, use the *show flash* command to confirm the presence of the new software image in flash.

```
!!!!!!!!!!!!!!!!!!!!!!!!!!!!!!!!!!!!!!!!!!!!!!!!!!!!!!!!!!!!!!
30468096 bytes copied in 101.540 secs (301664 bytes/sec)
ciscoasa# show flash
--#--  --length--  ----date/time------  path
  10   4096        Jul 29 2007 19:52:06  log
  18   4096        Jul 13 2010 11:02:44  coredumpinfo
  19   59          Mar 15 2011 14:44:34  coredumpinfo/coredump.cfg
  98   27629568    Sep 05 2014 20:17:42  asa904-k8.bin
  99   35634248    Nov 22 2014 01:21:24  anyconnect-win-3.1.05187-k9.pkg
 101   340         Nov 22 2014 14:40:04  RemoteUsers_client_profile.xml
  17   4096        Jul 29 2007 19:52:24  crypto_archive
 107   30468096    Nov 25 2014 15:19:53  asa922-4-k8.bin
 102   19884888    Nov 21 2014 05:49:26  asdm-731-101.bin

127111168 bytes total (12746752 bytes free)
ciscoasa#
ciscoasa#
```

Figure 46:
Viewing the new
software image in
flash memory

8. If you leave the old software version in flash, you must tell the ASA which version to use with the command *boot system disk0:asa922-4-k8.bin* (or whichever version you wish to use). I recommend leaving the old version in place, at least temporarily, as a backup in case of problems with the new version.

Hands-On Exercise 2.8:
Upgrading the ASDM Software in the Command Line Environment

In this exercise, you will upgrade the ASDM software image in the command line environment using a TFTP server.

Exercise Diagram

The exercise diagram is the same as used in the previous exercise.

Exercise Prerequisites

- The prerequisites are the same as used in the previous exercise, except that, instead of an ASA software image, you must have access to an upgraded version of the ASDM image. As with the previous exercise, you can download the most recent version from cisco.com, if you have a SMARTnet support contract.

- Also, as with the previous exercise, the ASDM software image must be located in the TFTP server's root directory, in my case c:\myconfigs.

- In my experience, if you're working with an ASA 5505, it is likely that you won't have enough room in flash memory for both the old and new versions of the ASDM image. Therefore, you should back up the existing version of ASDM software in case you need to erase it from flash memory before copying the new version to flash.

Exercise Steps

1. In the ASA's command line interface, issue the command show flash to check the amount of free memory available.

```
ciscoasa(config)#
ciscoasa(config)# show flash
--#--  --length--   -----date/time------  path
   10  4096         Jul 29 2007 19:52:06  log
   18  4096         Jul 13 2010 11:02:44  coredumpinfo
   19  59           Mar 15 2011 14:44:34  coredumpinfo/coredump.cfg
  102  27629568     Sep 05 2014 20:17:42  asa904-k8.bin
  103  35634248     Nov 22 2014 01:21:24  anyconnect-win-3.1.05187-k9.pkg
  112  25088760     Nov 25 2014 20:57:21  asdm-731.bin
  105  340          Nov 22 2014 14:40:04  RemoteUsers_client_profile.xml
   17  4096         Jul 29 2007 19:52:24  crypto_archive
  106  30468096     Nov 25 2014 15:19:52  asa922-4-k8.bin
  108  200          Nov 25 2014 15:29:22  upgrade_startup_errors_201411251529.log

127111168 bytes total (7544832 bytes free)
ciscoasa(config)#
```

Figure 47: Checking the amount of free memory

2. As you can see in the screen capture, 7544832 bytes of free memory are available. By checking the size of the new ASDM image in TFTPD64, you can see that the new image is 19884888 bytes in size.

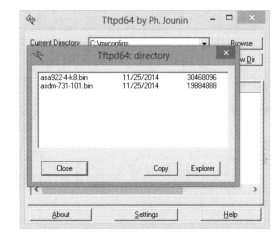

Figure 48:
Checking the size of the
image in the TFTP server

3. There's not enough room on this ASA for the new ASDM software without freeing up some space. If your ASA is similarly configured, use the command *del disk0:/asdm-731.bin* to remove the old ASDM image before installing the new one.

```
ciscoasa(config)#
ciscoasa(config)# del disk0:/asdm-731.bin

Delete filename [asdm-731.bin]?

Delete disk0:/asdm-731.bin? [confirm]

ciscoasa(config)#
```

Figure 49:
Deleting a file from flash memory

4. Once again, use the command *show flash* to view the contents of flash memory and you'll see that space is now available to install the new ASDM software image.

5. Use the command *copy tftp://192.168.1.5/asdm-731-101.bin flash* to copy the new image into flash memory (where 192.168.1.5 is the address of your computer running the TFTP server software).

```
ciscoasa(config)#
ciscoasa(config)# copy tftp://192.168.1.5/asdm-731-101.bin flash

Address or name of remote host [192.168.1.5]?

Source filename [asdm-731-101.bin]?

Destination filename [asdm-731-101.bin]?

Accessing tftp://192.168.1.5/asdm-731-101.bin...!!!!!!!!!!!!!!!!!!!!!
!!!!!!!!!!!!!!!!!!!!!!!!!!!!!!!!!!!!!!!!!!!!!!!!!!!!!!!!!!!!!!!!!!!!!!!!
!!!!!!!!!!!!!!!!!!!!!!!!!!!!!!!!!!!!!!!!!!!!!!!!!!!!!!!!!!!!!!!!!!!!!!!!
!!!!!!!!!!!!!!!!!!!!!!!!!!!!!!!!!!!!!!!!!!!!!!!!!!!!!!!!!!!!!!!!!!!!!!!!
!!!!!!!!!!!!!!!!!!!!!!!!!!!!!!!!!!!!!!!!!!!!!!!!!!!!!!!!!!!!!!!!!!!!!!!!
```

Figure 50: Copying the ASDM image into flash memory

6. If you have enough flash memory for both the old and new ASDM images and you want to specify which one to use, the command *asdm image disk0:/asdm-731-101.bin* can be used to choose the desired ASDM image. (Obviously, change the filename according to which image you want to use.)

Hands-On Exercise 2.9:
Upgrading Software Directly from Cisco in the ASDM

The ASDM allows you to upgrade software directly from Cisco including the ASA's software image (operating system) and the ASDM software by using your Cisco SMARTnet account. You can also use the ASDM to upgrade software from your local computer. The following steps cover upgrading directly from Cisco.com.

Note: Like all software vendors, Cisco makes slight changes in their software from one version to another. Your upgrade experience should be similar, but not necessarily identical to the steps shown in this exercise.

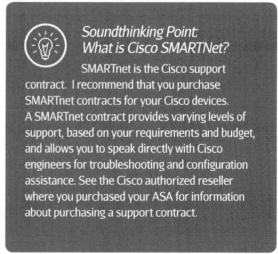

Soundthinking Point:
What is Cisco SMARTNet?

SMARTnet is the Cisco support contract. I recommend that you purchase SMARTnet contracts for your Cisco devices. A SMARTnet contract provides varying levels of support, based on your requirements and budget, and allows you to speak directly with Cisco engineers for troubleshooting and configuration assistance. See the Cisco authorized reseller where you purchased your ASA for information about purchasing a support contract.

Watch the Video

I have a video on my YouTube channel in which I demonstrate these procedures. Watch it at http://youtu.be/d9s7qpXJS4w.

Exercise Diagram

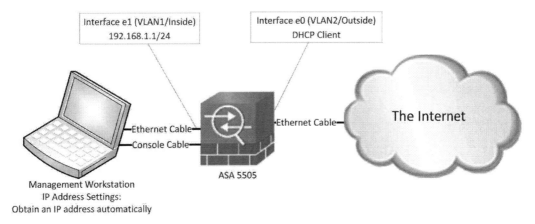

Figure 51: Diagram for installing software directly from Cisco.

Exercise Prerequisites

This exercise requires that you have a Cisco SMARTnet contract which allows you to download software for the ASA. If you don't have one, contact the Cisco authorized reseller where you purchased your ASA.

Exercise Steps

1. In the ASDM menu bar, click on Tools, then click on "Check for ASA/ASDM updates" (In earlier versions of the ASDM, the menu item was "Upgrade Software from Cisco.com ..."

Figure 52:
Upgrading software
in the ASDM

| Command Line Interface... |
| Show Commands Ignored by ASDM on Device |
| Packet Tracer... |
| Ping... |
| Traceroute... |
| File Management... |
| Check for ASA/ASDM Updates... |
| Upgrade Software from Local Computer... |
| Downgrade Software... |
| Backup Configurations |
| Restore Configurations |
| System Reload... |
| Administrator's Alert to Clientless SSL VPN Users... |
| Migrate Network Object Group Members... |
| Preferences... |
| ASDM Java Console... |

2. You'll be prompted for your Cisco.com username and password. Then, the Upgrade Wizard will appear. Click *Next*.

Figure 53:
Starting the upgrade process
in the ASDM

3. Depending on your current software versions, the wizard will offer you the appropriate upgrade options.

4. Select the desire option(s) and click *Next*.

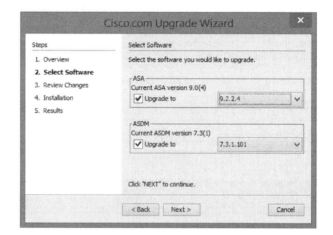

Figure 54:
Choosing versions for the upgrade

5. A confirmation window appears. Click *Next*.

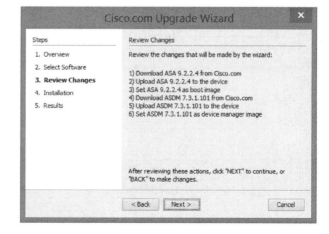

Figure 55:
Confirming details
of the upgrade

6. The download, upgrade, and cleanup process will take a few minutes.

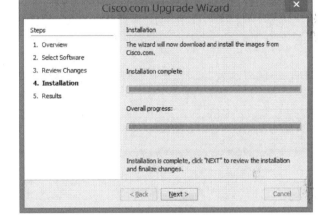

Figure 56:
Viewing the upgrade in progress

7. The progress bars will indicate when the installation process is complete. Click *Next*.

Figure 57:
The completed upgrade

8. Another window will appear confirming completion. Ensure the box labeled *Save configuration and reload device now* is checked. Click *Finish*.

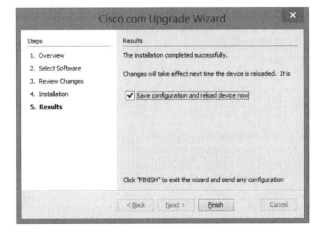

Figure 58:
Confirming a completed upgrade

9. If you have configured the ASDM to preview commands before sending them to the device, a window will appear showing two commands to be sent to the device. The first command tells the device to use the new ASDM image. The second command tells the device to use the new ASA software image. Click Send.

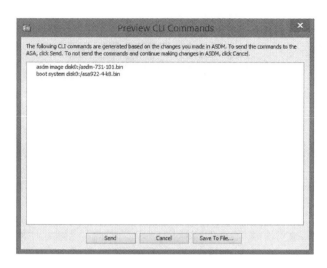

Figure 59:
Previewing upgrade commands

10. A Reload Status window appears notifying you that the device is shutting down.

11. Click Exit ASDM.

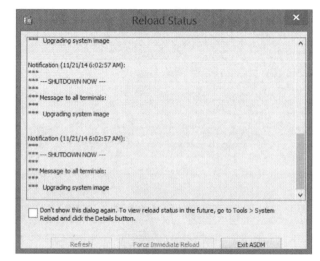

Figure 60:
Exiting from the upgrade process and reloading the ASA

12. When you re-connect to the ASDM, you can confirm the upgrade was successful in the Device Information window.

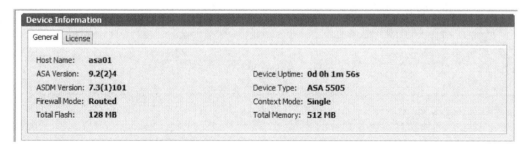

Figure 61: Confirming a successful upgrade in the ASDM

Hands-On Exercise 2.10:
Restore the ASA Software in a Fault Condition

In the following exercise, you will restore the ASA's software image as though you were in a catastrophic fault condition in which the software image had become corrupted or was missing.

Exercise Prerequisites

The prerequisites are the same as used in the previous exercise, except you may not need a Cisco SMARTnet contract if you're already backed up your ASA's software image.

Exercise Diagram

The exercise diagram is the same as used in the previous exercise.

Exercise Steps

In this exercise, you will work in ROM Monitor (ROMMON) mode. ROM Monitor mode is used for repairs and diagnostics.

1. Enter the following command to reload your security appliance:

    ```
    ciscoasa# reload

    System config has been modified. Save? [Y]es/[N]o: (choose Y to save
    any changes you made)

    Proceed with reload?[confirm] <Enter>
    ```

2. When you see the prompt to use BREAK or ESC to interrupt boot, press Esc to interrupt the boot process and enter rommon (ROM Monitor Mode).

3. In rommon, enter the following commands (note that the actual rommon prompt will include a line number, for example, rommon #3. You may also have to adjust the IP addresses and filename to reflect those in use on your network):

    ```
    rommon> interface ethernet 0/1 <Enter>

    MAC Address: XXXX.XXXX.XXXX

    Link is UP

    rommon> address 192.168.1.1 <Enter>

    rommon> server 192.168.1.2 <Enter>

    rommon> file asa911-k8.bin <Enter>
    ```

4. **Important:** Review the previous configuration to ensure that all information has been entered correctly and that the IP addresses listed in this document correspond to the actual IP addresses in use on your LAN segment. (If you happen to make a mistake, the security appliance will make 20 attempts to connect to the TFTP server before it times out.)

5. On your management workstation, use the *ipconfig* command to view its IP address. Notice that it no longer has an address on the 192.168.1.0 network and instead displays an address on the 169.254.0.0 network. This is due to your security appliance operating in ROM Monitor mode which does not support DHCP services. Manually assign the static IP address of 192.168.1.2 to your management workstation with a subnet mask of 255.255.255.0. It is not necessary to assign a default gateway nor any other IP parameters.

6. When you are satisfied that everything is correct, initiate the file transfer with the following command:

```
rommon> tftp <Enter>
```

(This procedure is considerably faster than backing up the software.)

7. Depending on your firewall's software version, you may have to enter the following command to boot your security appliance normally:

```
rommon> boot <Enter>
```

8. Reset your management workstation to obtain an IP address automatically.

9. You should see an IP address of 192.168.1.5 with a subnet mask of 255.255.255.0 and a default gateway of 192.168.1.1. If you do not see these values, type the command ipconfig /renew in the Command Line Interface window and press the Enter key. You should now see an IP address of 192.168.1.5 with a subnet mask of 255.255.255.0 and a default gateway of 192.168.1.1.

10. Confirm that the software was copied into the appliance's flash with the show flash command. (In the real world, if you had to do this, there would probably be size differences between the new and old files. In this exercise, you shouldn't be able to tell any difference.)

A Third-Party Software and Configuration Management Tool

If you're managing a large number of ASAs (and perhaps other devices, too), you may want to consider a third-party configuration management tool to centralize and automate the process. One tool that I've used successfully is Kiwi Cattools. There's a free version that supports a limited number of devices or a 30-day trial version. Both can be downloaded at http://www.solarwinds.com/kiwi-cattools.aspx.

CHAPTER 3:
Sending Logging Output to a Syslog Server

"Dance like it hurts, love like you need money, work when people are watching."

—Scott Adams

Using syslogd with the Security Appliance

Offloading logging information from network devices to a syslog server is generally considered best practice. Linux and UNIX systems include syslogd which can be configured to accept logging information from external sources. Windows systems, however, do not include a syslog service. Free tools such as tftpd32 (http://tftpd32.jounin.net) and Kiwi Syslog (http://www.kiwisyslog.com/free-edition.aspx) allow you to configure a computer running Microsoft Windows as a syslog server.

Syslog operates over UDP port 514.

There are eight levels of logging which determine the amount of information sent to the logging server.

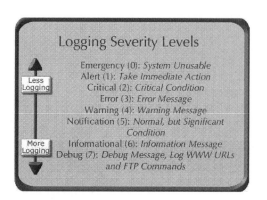

Figure 62:
Logging severity levels in syslog

Hands-On Exercise 3.1:
Sending Logging Output to a Syslog Server

In this exercise, you will configure and enable logging from your ASA security appliance to a syslog server.

Exercise Diagram

For this exercise, you will use a similar network configuration to that used in chapter one. Unlike chapter one, you must configure your management workstation to obtain an IP address automatically from the DHCP server running on the security appliance. You will connect your management workstation to the ASA security appliance using both the serial console cable and an Ethernet cable. It is also necessary to connect the outside interface to the public Internet using an Ethernet cable.

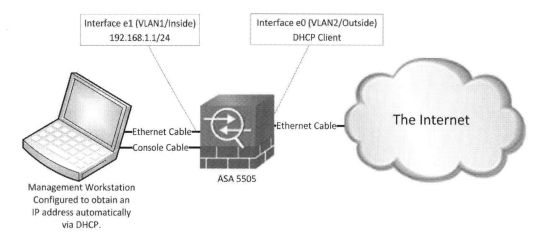

Figure 63: The network diagram for using syslog

The tftpd32 (or tftpd64) software you installed earlier includes a syslog server, similar to the UNIX syslogd daemon, a centralized logging server.

Enable Remote Logging

Enable remote logging on your security appliance with the following commands in *global configuration mode.*

1. Identify the syslog server:

   ciscoasa(config)# **logging host inside 192.168.1.5** <enter>

   (192.168.1.5 represents the IP address of your management workstation. It may be necessary to modify it if your management workstation's IP address is different.) I've noticed that sometimes I get an error message saying, "WARNING: configured logging host interface conflicts with route table entry". When I look at the device's routing table, I don't see anything that looks like a conflict. I've researched the error message, but haven't found a good reason for the warning and it doesn't seem to affect logging.

2. Configure the level of logging:

   ciscoasa(config)# **logging trap informational** <enter>

   (This is a fairly heavy level of logging which is appropriate for testing use, but would probably be too heavy for routine production use.)

3. Add timestamps to the logging entries:

   ciscoasa(config)# **logging timestamp** <enter>

   (syslog will include a timestamp based on the logging host time. You might, however, want to have the security appliance timestamp log entries based on the appliance' time.)

4. Tell the ASA to identify itself by its hostname in the logging entries:

   ciscoasa(config)# **logging device-id hostname** <enter>

5. Enable logging:

   ciscoasa(config)# **logging enable** <enter>

Test the Logging Configuration

6. Execute a ping to a non-existent address:

   ciscoasa(config)# **ping 172.16.1.1** <enter> (This assumes that there is no node at 172.16.1.1 in your network. In the unlikely event that you get a response, choose a different address that is not reachable in your network.)

7. Notice that Syslog records the attempted ping.

8. Change the logging level to warning and notice how much quieter syslog becomes:

   ciscoasa(config)# **logging trap warning** <enter>

If you'd like to customize tftpd32/tftpd64, perhaps to change default directories, you can do so by modifying the file tftpd32.ini (regardless of whether you're running the 32 or 64-bit version) found in either C:\Program Files\Tftpd64 or C:\Program Files (x86)\Tftpd32.

Now that you have made additional changes to your configuration, save it to flash memory and back it up to your TFTP server using the procedures you learned earlier. (Hint: You can use the simple command wr to write the configuration to flash memory. It is the same as `copy running-config startup-config`.)

ciscoasa# **wr**

ciscoasa# **copy run tftp://192.168.1.5/config _ syslog.txt** <enter>
(where 192.168.1.5 is the IP address of the management workstation containing your TFTP server)

Note: As you have probably noticed, tftpd32 (tftpd64) is a very basic syslog server with limited features. There are commercial products such as KiwiSyslog offering a much more extensive feature set. Configuration of the ASA is the same, regardless of your choice of syslog server.

Soundthinking Point:
When syslog does not work

If syslog does not seem to be receiving logging information

- Ensure that it is enabled on your ASA with the command "logging enable"
- Ensure that your Windows firewall permits syslog traffic (it's usually on UDP port 514)
- Check for a conflict on UDP port 514, such as another logging server running

CHAPTER 4:
Remote Management Options

*"The question of whether computers can think is just like
the question of whether submarines can swim."*

--Edsger W. Dijkstra

Remote Console Access

There are two options for remote CLI access: Telnet and SSH (Secure Shell). You cannot Telnet to the lowest security interface (typically the outside interface) except through a VPN tunnel. In any case, SSH is a better choice, even on an internal network, due to the encryption imposed by SSH and the absence of any encryption with Telnet. If you must use Telnet, assume that everyone on the network is seeing the entire session in plain text including usernames and passwords.

Note: A free video demonstrating the non-secure nature of Telnet is available on the soundtraining.net YouTube channel at http://youtu.be/loiIh9ui26I.

Telnet

Telnet operates over TCP port 23. Virtually all modern operating systems include a Telnet client. On computers running recent versions of the Windows operating system, Telnet is not installed by default and must be enabled by using the option to *Turn Windows features on or off* under Control Panel\ Programs\Programs and Features. Usually, you can start the Telnet client by opening a CLI session and simply typing, "telnet [target hostname or IP address". In order to permit incoming Telnet connections, you must first tell the security appliance which host(s) and/or networks are permitted to connect, set a Telnet password, and optionally set a Telnet timeout (the default is five minutes):

`telnet 192.168.16.0 255.255.255.0 inside` would allow all hosts on the 192.168.16.0/24 network to connect with Telnet to the security appliance's inside interface.

`telnet 192.168.16.1 255.255.255.255 inside` would allow only the host at 192.168.16.1 to connect with Telnet to the security appliance's inside interface.

`password [telnet password]` (This password is also used for SSH sessions)

`telnet timeout 20` would set an idle timeout value of 20 minutes.

You can configure a local database of usernames and passwords or configure the security appliance to connect to an authentication server to authenticate Telnet users. On an ASA running software earlier than version 8.4, if no pre-configured username exists for Telnet sessions, the default username is *pix* and the password is *cisco*. On later versions, the default username is no longer supported.

SSH (Secure Shell)

There are two versions of SSH (version 1 and version 2). Both operate over TCP port 22. Both are supported on the Cisco security appliance. Unlike Telnet, SSH provides strong authentication and encryption. SSH usernames can be up to 100 characters in length and SSH passwords can be up to 50 characters in length.

Configuration of SSH is similar to that for Telnet, but you must also configure a hostname (if one does not already exist), identify the security appliance's domain, and generate an RSA key with the following commands:

`hostname asa01`

`domain-name soundtraining.net`

`crypto key generate rsa modulus 1024` (where *modulus* represents the key and *1024* is the key size. Larger keys are more difficult to crack, but take longer to generate. As of this writing in early 2015, Cisco recommends a modulus size of 1024.)

`ssh 192.168.1.0 255.255.255.0 inside` would allow all hosts on the 192.168.1.0/24 network to connect with SSH to the security appliance's inside interface.

`ssh 192.168.1.1 255.255.255.255 inside` would allow only the host at 192.168.1.1 to connect with SSH to the security appliance's inside interface.

`password [ssh password]` (Telnet and SSH sessions use the same password. Remember, if you use Telnet, the password is sent as clear text.)

`ssh timeout 20` sets an idle timeout value of 20 minutes.

You can have a maximum of five SSH clients in simultaneous sessions on the Cisco security appliance console.

Hands-On Exercise 4.1:
Configuring and Using Telnet

Exercise Diagram

For this exercise, you will use a similar network configuration to that used in earlier chapters.

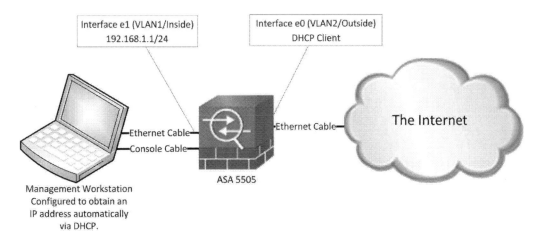

Figure 64: The network idagram for using Telnet and SSH

Exercise Prerequisites

This exercise requires you to have the PuTTY software installed on your computer. If you don't have it, it's available for free at www.putty.org.

Exercise Steps

These steps must be done in a console session via your serial console cable.

1. Begin by configuring the address(es) from which the Adaptive Security Appliance will accept connections:

```
ciscoasa> en <enter>

Password: p@ss5678 <enter>

ciscoasa# config t <enter>

ciscoasa(config)# telnet 192.168.1.0 255.255.255.0 inside <enter>
```

(where "192.168.1.0" represents your inside network address based on your firewall's current configuration. If your firewall is configured differently, adjust your settings as needed. Remember to use commands like show ip and show interface to get the necessary information to complete this exercise.)

2. Configure a password for Telnet access:

```
ciscoasa(config)# passwd cisco <enter>
```

3. Telnet sessions have a default timeout value of five minutes. Set your appliance timeout value to four minutes with this command:

```
ciscoasa(config)# telnet timeout 4 <enter>
```

Hands-On Exercise 4.2:
Testing the Telnet Configuration

In this exercise, you will test your configuration by attempting to establish a Telnet session from your management workstation using PuTTY.

Exercise Diagram

This exercise uses the same diagram as the previous exercise.

Exercise Prerequisites

This exercise has the same prerequisites as the previous exercise.

Exercise Steps

1. Open PuTTY (if you already have PuTTY open, right-click on the title bar and choose *New Session* ...

2. In the Host Name (or IP address) field, enter the IP address of your ASA's inside interface (192.168.1.1).

3. Log on with the password cisco. If the connection is not successful, review your settings paying particular attention to typographical errors. Make certain that the statement in which you tell the ASA which addresses to accept is correctly configured for your inside network and that you specified the inside interface.

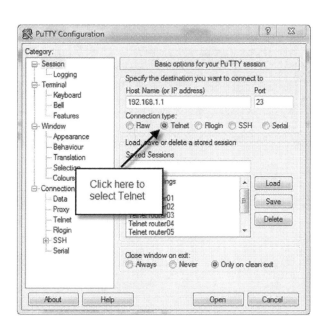

Figure 65: Staring a Telnet connection in PuTTY

Hands-On Exercise 4.3:
Configuring and Using SSH (Secure Shell)

In this exercise, you will configure SSH on your appliance. You will then attempt to connect to the appliance using SSH.

Exercise Diagram

This exercise uses the same diagram as the previous exercise.

Exercise Prerequisites

This exercise has the same prerequisites as the previous exercise.

Exercise Steps

1. Generate an RSA keypair with the following command:

   ```
   asa(config)# crypto key generate rsa modulus 1024 <enter>
   ```

   (The modulus represents the key length, in this case 1024 bits.)

2. The firewall will ask if you want to replace the existing RSA keypair. Confirm by entering **yes**.

3. As with Telnet, you must specify the address(es) from which your appliance will accept inbound connections:

   ```
   asa(config)# ssh 192.168.0.0 255.255.0.0 inside <enter>
   ```

   (This statement will allow any host whose IP address begins with 192.168 to connect via SSH to your firewall's inside interface. In a real world setting, a more restrictive configuration would be appropriate.)

4. In the past, PIX firewalls and ASA security appliances used a default username of *pix* if no username was configured. Starting with software version 8.4, a username and password must be explicitly configured with the following command:

   ```
   ciscoasa(config)# username testuser password p@ss1234 <enter>
   ```

5. Enable AAA authentication for SSH with the following command:

   ```
   asa(config)# aaa authentication ssh console LOCAL
   ```

6. Set the timeout value to four minutes for SSH connections:

   ```
   asa(config)# ssh timeout 4 <enter>
   ```

7. When you are finished, save the configuration to flash memory:

   ```
   asa(config)# write memory <enter>
   ```

Hands-On Exercise 4.4:
Test the SSH Configuration

Exercise Diagram
This exercise uses the same diagram as the previous exercise.

Exercise Prerequisites
This exercise has the same prerequisites as the previous exercise.

Exercise Steps
Attempt to connect to your appliance by using PuTTY:

1. Open PuTTY (if you already have PuTTY open, right-click on the title bar and choose *New Session* …

2. Ensure that the radio button labeled SSH is selected in the PuTTY window. In the field labeled Host Name (or IP address), enter the inside IP address of your security appliance. Click the button labeled Open.

3. In the Security Warning window that appears, click Yes to accept the key. (On a production system, you should confirm that you are connecting to the system you intended to before accepting the key.)

4. Log on with the username *testuser* and the password *p@ss1234*. If the connection is not successful, confirm that you have correctly entered the username and password. Review your appliances configuration using privileged mode commands such as *show run ssh*.

5. Now that you have made additional changes to your configuration, save it to flash memory and back it up to your TFTP server using the procedures you learned earlier:

    asa# **wr** <enter>

    asa# **copy run tftp://192.168.1.5/config _ ssh.txt** <enter>

    (where 192.168.1.5 is the IP address of your TFTP server)

Configuring and Managing Remote Management through ASDM

As mentioned previously, ASDM is the Adaptive Security Device Manager. It is the graphical user interface through which you can configure and manage your security appliance.

Traditionally, most system engineers prefered to manage systems in the command-line interface (CLI) due to the extensive command set available and the freedom to operate the device according to individual preferences. Although those benefits continue to exist, modern graphical user interfaces (GUI) offer an increasingly expanding range of commands and the significant benefit of preventing syntax errors. I try not to limit myself to using one particular management tool, rather, I use whichever tools help me do my job better and more efficiently.

In order to use ASDM, you must specify which host(s) are allowed to access the security appliance via HTTP with the following command:

```
asa01(config)#
asa01(config)# http 192.168.0.0 255.255.0.0 inside
asa01(config)# http server enable
asa01(config)#
```

Figure 66: Enabling web management (ASDM) on an inside interface

In the above example, all hosts connected to the inside interface with an IP address beginning with 192.168 are allowed to use ASDM. You can narrow the authorized hosts by using a longer subnet mask. For example, if you want to allow only hosts whose IP address begins with 192.168.130, you would use the statement **http 192.168.130.0 255.255.255.0 inside**.

In order to use ASDM, you must connect to the security appliance using Secure HTTP: **https://192.168.1.1**

You can run ASDM either through a browser or install it as a Java applet on your computer.

CHAPTER 5:
Logon Banners and Authentication, Authorization, and Accounting

"The real danger is not that computers will begin to think like men,
but that men will begin to think like computers."

--Sydney J. Harris

Configuring Banners

Banners can be configured to display when a user first connects (MOTD), when a user logs in (login), or when a user accesses privileged mode (exec). Banners are used for legal warnings such as cautioning a user not to access a restricted system or that access of a system is subject to monitoring and logging. Banners are also used on locked systems placed at customer locations by a service provider to provide contact information for technical support. The Cisco security appliance supports the use of login banners in console sessions and Telnet sessions, but not in SSH sessions. Exec and MOTD banners are supported in console, Telnet, and SSH sessions. Banners can also be configured for use with ASDM sessions.

Here is how banners are displayed:

MOTD

When usernames are not configured, MOTD displays at login in a serial console session and before login in Telnet sessions.

When usernames are configured, MOTD displays before login in a Telnet session and after login in a serial console session.

Login

The login banner displays before login in Telnet and serial console sessions. It also displays upon login in ASDM sessions.

Exec

The exec banner displays before the device displays the enable prompt..

ASDM

The asdm banner displays immediately following login in an ASDM session. The user must click Continue or Disconnect. This banner can be used to require users to accept the terms of a policy before continuing.

Figure 67:
An ASDM banner.

How to Configure a Banner

To configure a banner, use the following configuration mode commands:

`asa(config)#`**`banner motd This is a restricted system.`**

`asa(config)#`**`banner motd Do not attempt unauthorized access.`**

Notice the use of two banner motd statements to create a multi-line banner.

You can view the banners you created with the privileged mode command *show running-config banner.*

Hands-On Exercise 5.1:
Creating CLI Banners on the Security Appliance

In the following exercise, you will create MOTD, login, and EXEC banners. After configuring the banners, you will test the configuration by logging on in different ways to observe which banners display.

Exercise Diagram

For this exercise, you will use a similar network configuration to that used in earlier chapters.

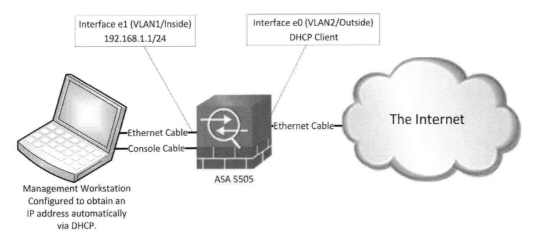

Figure 68: The network diagram for configuring banners

Exercise Prerequisites

The prerequisites for this exercise are the same as in the previous exercise.

Exercise Steps

1. In *global configuration mode*, enter the following commands:

   ciscoasa(config)# **banner motd This is the MOTD banner** <enter>
   ciscoasa(config)# **banner login This is the login banner** <enter>
   ciscoasa(config)# **banner exec This is the EXEC banner** <enter>

2. Display the banners you just created with the following command:

   ciscoasa(config)# **show run banner** <enter>

3. Type exit repeatedly until you are logged out of your security appliance.

Hands-On Exercise 5.2:
Test the Banner Configuration

1. In a serial console session, notice which banners are displayed with the login prompt.

2. Enter privileged mode and notice which banners are displayed.

3. From your management workstation, start a Telnet session and again observe which banners are displayed. When you are finished, exit the Telnet session.

4. Also from your management workstation, start an SSH session to observe which banners are displayed. If the SSH session fails, review your configuration to see if you can identify the cause of the problem.

5. When you are finished, exit the SSH session.

6. Backup your configuration to your TFTP server using the procedures learned previously.

    ```
    ciscoasa# wr <enter>

    ciscoasa# copy run tftp://192.168.1.5/config _ banners.txt <enter>
    ```

    (where 192.168.1.5 is the IP address of your TFTP server)

Hands-On Exercise 5.3:
Configuring an ASDM Banner

Exercise Diagram

The diagram for this exercise is the same as the previous exercise.

Exercise Prerequisites

The prerequisites for this exercise are the same as in the previous exercise.

Exercise Steps

In this exercise, you will configure a banner which will be displayed upon successful login in the ASDM. It can be used as a security warning, to require acceptance of a terms of access policy, or for any other purpose requiring a banner.

1. In global configuration mode, use the following command to create an ASDM banner:
    ```
    ciscoasa(conifg)#banner asdm This is a restricted and monitored system.
    By clicking Continue, you indicate your acceptance of the corporate
    terms of access policy located at www.corpname.com/toa.
    ```

```
asa01(config)#
asa01(config)# banner asdm This is a restricted and monitored system. By click$
asa01(config)#
```

Figure 69: Configuring an ASDM banner

Notice, in the screen capture, how the dollar symbol ($) at the end of the line indicates that the text has been scrolled to the right and the end of the command is hidden.

2. Test the configuration by logging in to the device using the ASDM.

You can also configure banners in the ASDM. Go to Configuration>Device Management>Management Access>Command Line (CLI)>Banner.

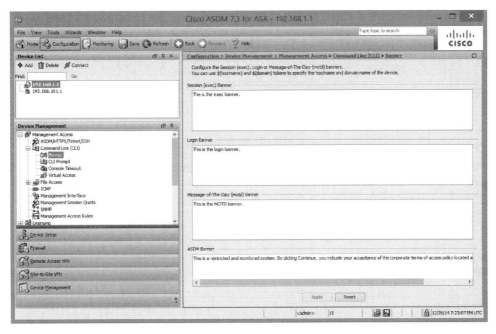

Figure 70: Configuring banners in the ASDM

Displaying and Clearing Banners

You can show all banners on the device by using the following command:

```
show run banner
```

You can remove all banners from the device by using the following command:

```
clear configure banner
```

Configuring Authentication, Authorization, and Accounting (AAA)

As discussed previously, AAA (Authentication, Authorization, and Accounting) is a means of identifying who is entering a system or network, what that individual is allowed to do, and what they did while on the system or network.

- Authentication
    - Proving that you are who you say you are
    - Authentication is accomplished by passing at least one of three tests
        - Something you know such as a password or a PIN
        - Something you have such as a smart card or a token
        - Something you are such as your fingerprint, your voice, or your face

Increasingly, security best practices require two-factor authentication using two of the above tests. For example, your ATM might require you to use a smart card (something you have) combined with a PIN (something you know).

- Authorization
    - What you can do

- Accounting
    - What you did

The Cisco security appliance family supports several means of implementing AAA:

AAA can be implemented on an external server, thus centralizing AAA for many appliances and minimizing the impact of AAA on system resources on any one device.

Remote Authentication Technologies

When implemented through an external server, several different technologies can be used, including:

- RADIUS—RADIUS is the Remote Authentication Dial-In User Service. RADIUS is an industry standard authentication technology that is widely supported on many different platforms, including Windows, Linux and UNIX.

- TACACS+—TACACS+ stands for Terminal Access Controller Access Control System Plus. It was developed by Cisco as an alternative to RADIUS. TACACS+ divides the authentication and authorization components into separate transmissions.

RADIUS and TACACS+ can both be used for system management access, plus VPN access.

The following technologies are available to manage VPN access:

- SDI—SDI is RSA SecurID. SDI uses a username and single-use password to authenticate end users or applications for VPN authentication.

- NTLMv1—NTLMv1 allows VPN authentication through the use of Microsoft Windows NTLM version 1.

- Kerberos—Kerberos is an authentication technology developed at MIT based on trusted third parties. Kerberos is the authentication technology used in Microsoft Active Directory networks. Kerberos supports the use of several popular encryption methods including DES, 3DES, and RC4. Kerberos is supported on the security appliance as a means of authenticating end-users for VPN access.

- LDAP—LDAP is Lightweight Directory Access Protocol. LDAP is the directory structure technology upon which Microsoft's Active Directory is based. The Cisco security appliance supports LDAP for VPN authentication through the use of tunnel-groups.

Local database

In situations where there is only a single device to be maintained, you may prefer to use a local user database for AAA. Additionally, it is a good idea to have a local user database as a fallback in the event of a AAA server failure or network failure that would prevent access to the remote server. In the following exercise, you will configure several usernames and grant various levels of privilege to those users.

Hands-On Exercise 5.4:
Configuring Usernames and Local Authentication

Configuring usernames is part of implementing AAA (Authentication, Authorization, and Accounting) in that you can specify who can gain access to the security appliance, what they are allowed to do, and later review what they did. In this exercise, you will configure usernames in the local database and specify levels of access.

Building the Configuration in the ASDM

1. On your management workstation, click on Start, then click on Run. In the Run dialog window, enter *https://192.168.1.1* (where 192.168.1.1 is your ASA's inside interface address) and press Enter. (Note the use of "s" in the protocol, identifying the connection as requiring SSL security.)

2. Use a blank username and the password *p@ss5678*. Click through the security warnings to open the ASDM.

3. Ensure that ASDM is configured to allow you to preview commands before sending them to the device by clicking on the *Tools* menu in the menu bar of ASDM. Click on *Preferences* and confirm that the box labeled *Preview commands before sending them to the device* is checked.

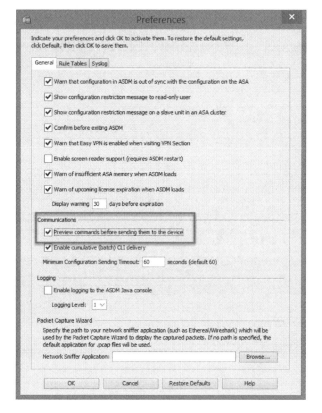

Figure 71:
Setting ASDM to preview commands

4. In the ASDM console menu, click on *Configuration*. On the menu on the left side of the window, click on *Device Management*. Expand *Users/AAA* and click on *User Accounts*.

5. In the *User Accounts* window, click on *Add*.

6. In the *Add User Account* window, change the default username to *user3*. Enter the password *p@ss1234* and confirm it.

7. Under *Access Restriction*, set the privilege level to 3 and click *OK*.

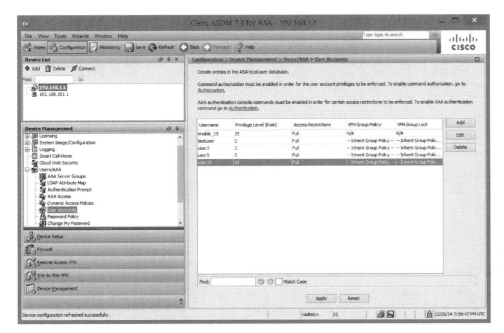

Figure 72:
Adding a user in the ASDM

8. Repeat steps 6 and 7, changing the default username to *user5*. Enter the password *p@ss1234* and confirm it.

9. Set the privilege level for user5 to *5*.

10. Repeat steps 6 and 7 again, this time changing the default username to *user15*. Enter the password *p@ss1234* and confirm it.

11. Set the privilege level for user15 to *15*.

12. When you are finished, at the bottom of the *User Accounts* window, click *Apply*. In the *Preview CLI Commands* window, review the changes and click *Send* to send the changes to the appliance.

13. When you're finished, the ASDM should look like this:

Figure 73:
New users in
the ASDM

Note, in the screen capture, that you can see the user *enable_15*, a default user, and *testuser*, the user added earlier for the SSH exercise, in addition to the three users added in this exercise.

In order to enforce authentication, you must also make the following changes:

14. Under *Device Management>Users/AAA* (on the left-hand side of your screen), select *AAA Access*.

15. On the *Authentication* tab, check the box labeled *Enable* to require authentication for administrator access to the appliance. Accept the default *Server Group Local*.

16. In the *Require authentication for the following types of connections* section, check the boxes labeled *SSH* and *Telnet* and accept the default *Server Group Local*. (In a real-world setting, you would probably want to enforce authentication for ASDM as well.)

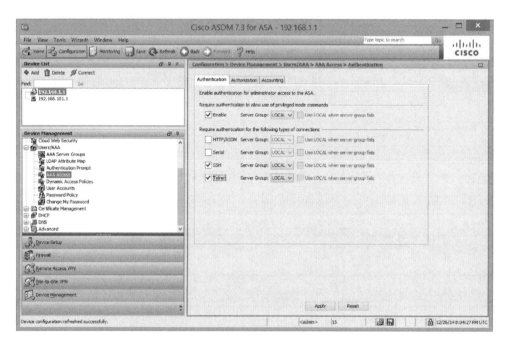

Figure 74: Configuring AAA authentication in the ASDM

17. At the bottom of the window, click on *Apply*. In the *Preview CLI Commands* window, review the changes and click *Send* to send the changes to the appliance.

18. Under the *Authorization* tab, in the section labeled *Enable authorization for ASA command access*, check the box labeled *Enable* and click on the button labeled *Set ASDM Defined User Roles*.

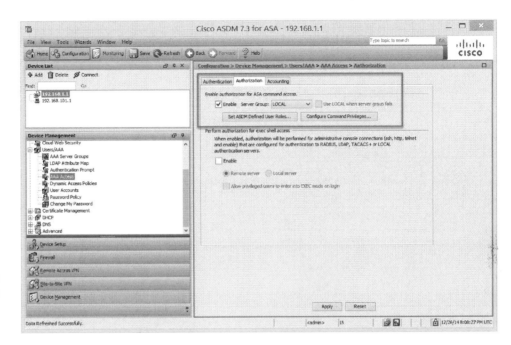

Figure 75:
Enabling command
authorization

19. The *ASDM Defined User Roles* window will appear. Notice that it associates various commands in the three left-hand columns with privilege levels displayed in the far right-hand column. The privilege levels represent *Monitor (level 3), Read Only (level 5)*, and *Admin (level 15)*. Level 15 commands are not displayed because Admin already has full access. When you have finished reviewing the settings, click *Yes* to allow ASDM to configure commands with the indicated privilege levels.

Be sure to click *Apply* and *Send* to send the commands to the security appliance.

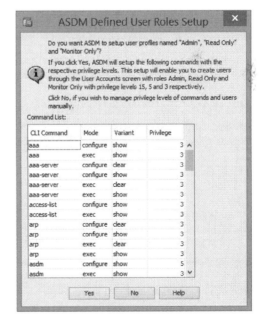

Figure 76:
Configuring command authorization in the ASDM

(Note: In a real world setting, you could use this tool to set very specific access-levels for users at any command level.)

Hands-On Exercise 5.5:
Testing the Configuration

1. Use PuTTY to open an SSH session to the ASA. (Use PuTTY to connect to 192.168.1.1.)

2. Notice that it now prompts you for a username. Enter *user3* with the password *p@ss1234*.

3. You are logged in to the device in User Mode. Enter *enable* and the password *p@ss1234* to change to Privileged Mode.

4. Enter the command *show running-config*. What happens?

5. The command should fail with an invalid input error because user3 is associated with command level three and command level three does not include authorization to run the *show running-config* command.

6. Type *exit* to close PuTTY. Re-open the SSH session to 192.168.1.1, but this time, enter the username *user5* with the password *p@ss1234*.

7. Enter *enable* and the password *p@ss1234* to change to Privileged Mode.

8. Enter the command *show running-config*. What happens now?

9. The command should be successful, because user5 is associated with command level five and command level five includes authorization to run the *show running-config* command.

10. Enter the command *config t*. What happens?

11. The command should fail with an invalid input error because user5 is associated with command level five and command level five does not include authorization to run the *configure terminal* command.

12. Type *exit* to close the PuTTY SSH session. Re-open it as before, but this time, enter the username *user15* with the password *p@ss1234*.

13. Enter *enable* and the password *p@ss1234* to change to Privileged Mode.

14. Enter the command *show running-config*. What happens now?

15. The command should be successful, because user15 is associated with command level fifteen and command level fifteen includes authorization to run the *show running-config* command.

16. Enter the command *config t*. What happens now?

17. The command should be successful, because user15 is associated with command level fifteen and command level fifteen includes authorization to run the *configure terminal* command.

18. Now that you have made additional changes to your configuration, save it to flash memory and back it up to your TFTP server using the procedures you learned earlier.

```
ciscoasa# wr <enter>

ciscoasa# copy run tftp://192.168.1.5/config _ aaa _ priv.txt <enter>
```

(where 192.168.1.5 is the IP address of your TFTP server)

How to Use Active Directory to Authenticate RADIUS Users

RADIUS (Remote Authentication Dial-In User Service) is a fairly old protocol, as indicated by its name. It is still widely available and widely used for centralizing authentication services. With Cisco devices, RADIUS can be used to authenticate VPN users, SSH/Telnet users, ASDM users, and even serial console users. The Cisco ASA supports several remote authentication options in addition to RADIUS, including TACACS+, HTML forms, RSA SecureID, Kerberos, and LDAP. Of course, local authentication is also supported and is usually recommended as a fallback in case of network or server outages.

In the following exercise, you will install RADIUS on a computer running Windows Server 2012 and learn how to configure a Cisco ASA Security Appliance to support RADIUS authentication.

Hands-On Exercise 5.6:
How to Configure RADIUS on a Windows Server 2012 Computer

Exercise Diagram

There is no diagram for this exercise. The steps do not require a network for completion.

Prerequisites

A computer running Windows Server 2012 with Active Directory Domain Services installed and an Active Directory user account with administrator privileges.

Watch the Video

There is a video on my YouTube channel in which I demonstrate the following procedures. Watch the video at http://youtu.be/1yYywwPWXys.

Exercise Steps

1. On Windows Server 2012, RADIUS runs as part of the Network Policy and Access Server role.

2. On the computer running Windows Server 2012, launch the Server Manager and navigate to Local Server. In the upper right-hand corner, click Manage and select *Add Roles and Features*.

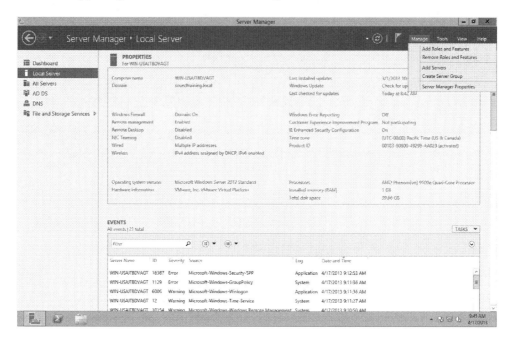

Figure 77: Windows Server 2012 Server Manager

3. Skip the initial welcome page and accept the default on the *Role based or feature based installation* page.

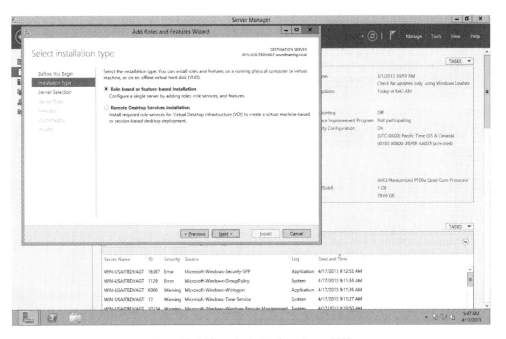

Figure 78: Adding roles in Windows Server 2012

4. Select the destination server from the list.

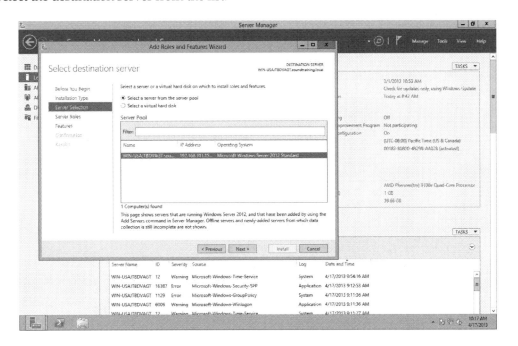

Figure 79: Choosing the destination server for a new role

5. Add *Network Policy and Access Server* and click through the prompts to return to this screen and click *Next.*

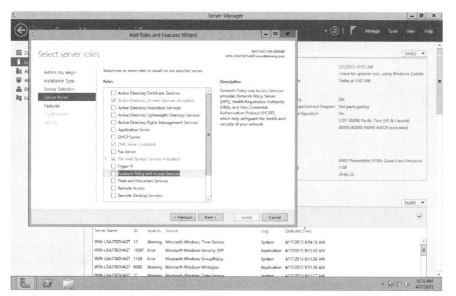

Figure 80:
Selecting server roles

6. Click through the next few screens until you get to a button labeled *Install.* Click it.

Figure 81:
Confirming Windows
Server 2012 installation
selections

7. Your computer will run for several minutes doing the installation. When it's finished, click *Close*.

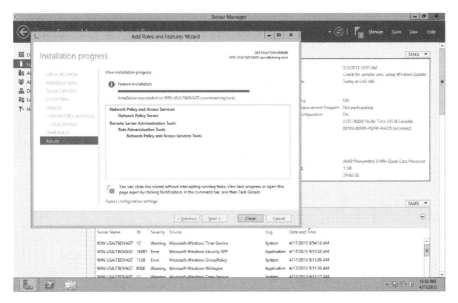

Figure 82:
The Add Roles and
Features Wizard

8. In the Server Manager, in the list on the left-hand side, select *NAP*. The NAP server will appear in the large window. Right-click on the server and, on the context menu, choose *Network Policy Server*.

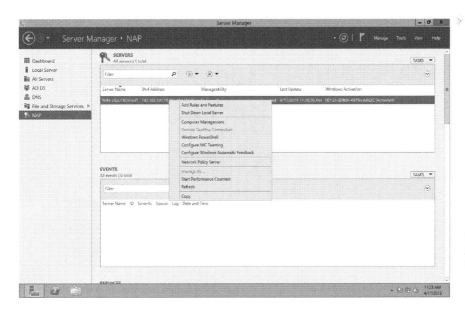

Figure 83:
Adding the Network
Policy Server

9. A Microsoft Management Console will appear. In the console, right-click NPS (at the top of the list on the left) and, in the context-menu, click *Register the server in Active Directory*.

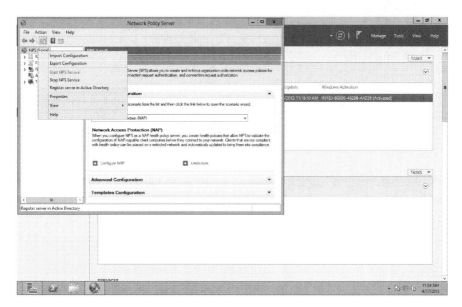

Figure 84:
Registering the
Network Policy Server
in Active Directory

10. Click through the various prompts. Then, back in the Microsoft Management Console, expand *RADIUS*, right-click on *RADIUS clients*, and choose *New*.

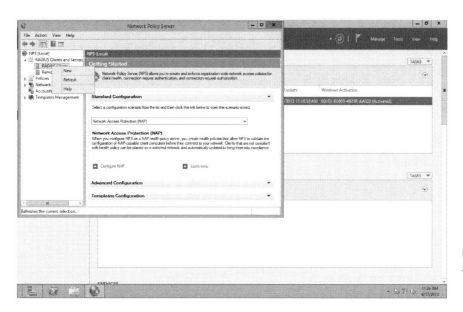

Figure 85:
Adding RADIUS clients

11. Give the firewall a friendly name (be sure to write it down, because you'll need it later). Enter its IP address and the shared secret (the key you'll use in the aaa-server group on the ASA Security Appliance. Write this down, too, because you won't be able to see it later if you forget and it must match the key on the ASA.). Click OK.

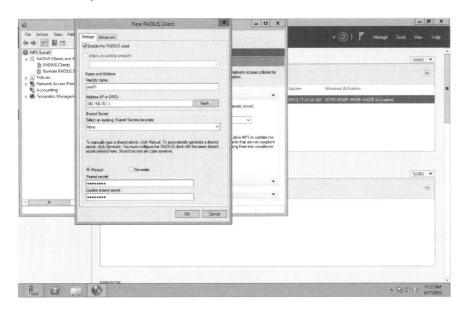

Figure 86:
Setting up the shared secret

12. Now, back in the MMC, expand *Policies* and right-click on *Connection Request Policies*, and choose *New*.

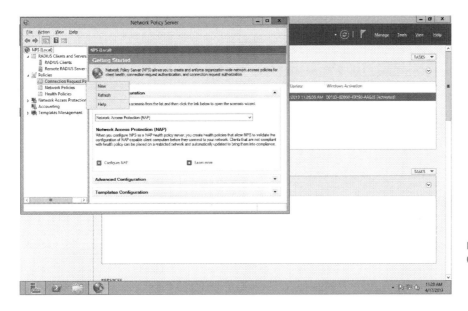

Figure 87:
Creating a new policy

13. Give the policy a descriptive name and click the button labeled *Next*.

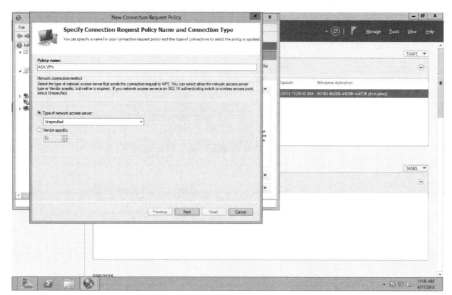

Figure 88:
Naming the new policy

14. Click *Add* and, in the next window, choose *Client Friendly Name*. Click *Add*.

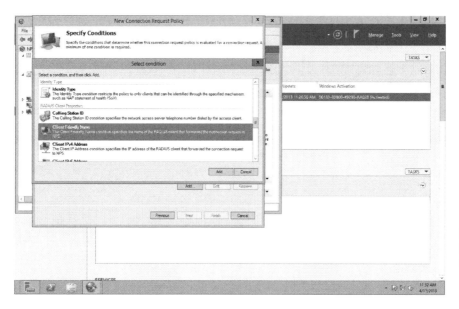

Figure 89:
Selecting a new
client policy

15. Enter the friendly name you created earlier, click *OK*, and click *Next*.

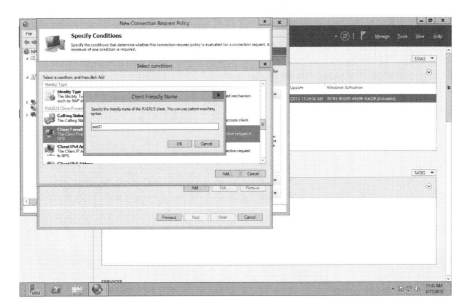

Figure 90:
Choosing the
friendly name of the
RADIUS client

16. Click through the next couple of windows until you get to the *Configure Settings* window. Change the attribute to *User-Name* and click *Next*.

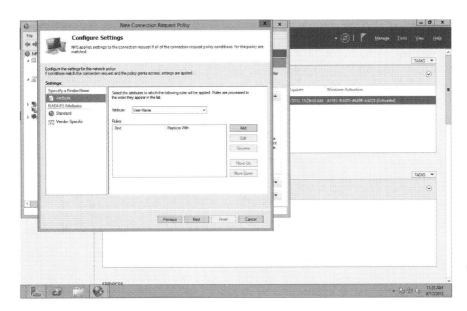

Figure 91:
Changing the attribute

17. In the *Completing Connection Request Policy Wizard* window, click *Finish*.

18. In the *Network Policy Server* MMC, right-click on *Network Policies* and choose *New*.

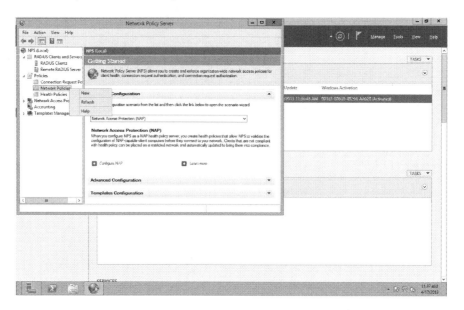

Figure 92: Creating a new network policy

19. Give the policy a name and click *Next*

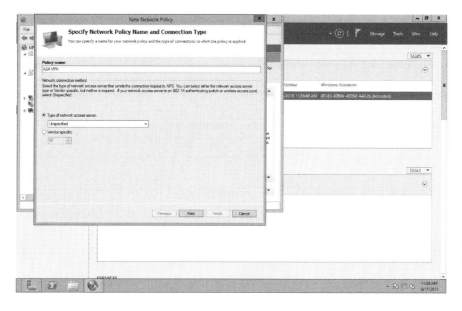

Figure 93:
Naming the new policy

20. Click *Add* and, in the *Specify Conditions* window, choose *User Groups*.

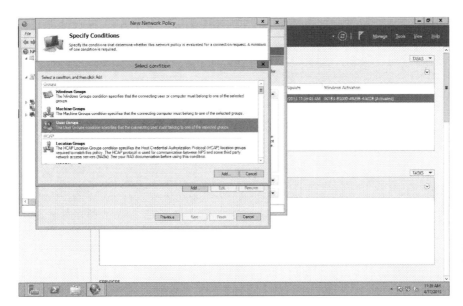

Figure 94:
Specifying conditions
for the network policy

21. Click *Add*, then choose the Active Directory Security Group whose members you want to grant access to the VPN. (In the example, I just allowed all Domain Users, but you might want to narrow it down to a smaller group.) Click *OK* and *Next*.

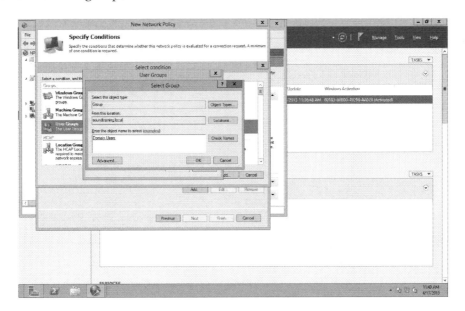

Figure 95: Choosing the AD security group

22. On the *Specify Access Permission* page, click *Next* to accept the default.

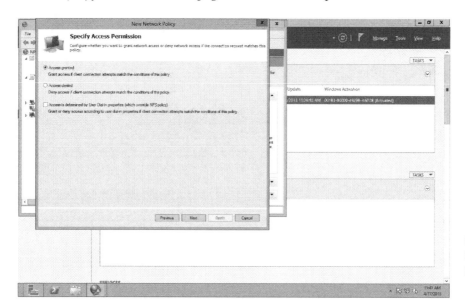

Figure 96:
Specifying access
permissions

23. On the *Configure Authentication Methods* page, check the box labeled *Unencrypted Authentication PAP SPAP* and click *Next*.

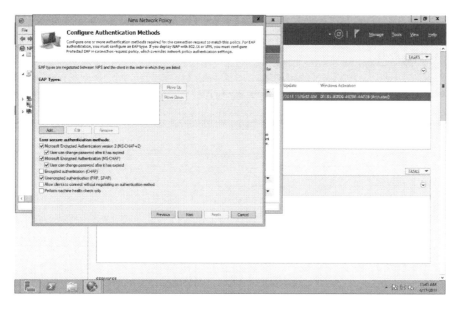

Figure 97:
Choosing the
authentication
methods

24. Click No on the *Connection Request Policy* warning, click *Next* on the next two pages until you get to the final page. Click the *Finish* button.

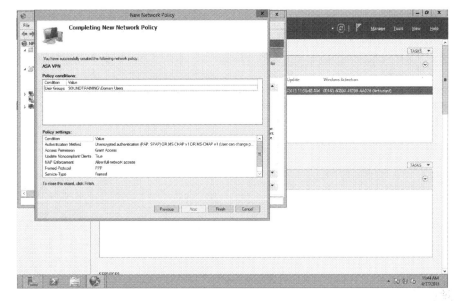

Figure 98:
Completing the Windows
Server 2012 configuration

The installation of the RADIUS server on your computer running Windows Server 2012 is now complete.

Hands-On Exercise 5.7:
Configuring SSH Authentication through Active Directory

In this exercise, you will configure your ASA security appliance to authenticate SSH users against a Microsoft Active Directory domain controller.

Exercise Diagram

This exercise requires the addition of a computer (virtual or physical) running Windows Server 2012, configured as an Active Directory Domain Controller.

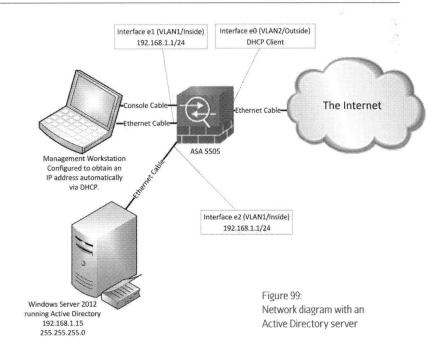

Figure 99:
Network diagram with an
Active Directory server

Exercise Prerequisites

- A Windows domain controller configured with Network Policy and Access Server role and the Network Policy Server (for more information, including a step-by-step guide, see the preceding exercise in this book).

- An Active Directory user account on the Windows domain controller for user01 with a password of p@ss1234

- A local user account which should have been configured previously

- User user01's Dial-In Remote Access permission on the Windows domain controller must be set to *Allow Access*.

Exercise Steps

There are two parts to configuring the ASA to authenticate through Active Directory: You must create the server-group and identify the authentication protocol to be used and you must identify the services which will use the remote authentication.

1. In a terminal window, enter *global configuration mode*:

   ```
   ciscoasa>en
   Password: p@ss5678
   ciscoasa# conf t
   ciscoasa(config)#
   ```

2. In global configuration mode, specify the authentication protocol (radius), create the authentication group (RADIUSSERVERS), identify the interface to which the authentication server is connected (outside), specify the server's IP address, and the key shared between the security appliance and the authentication server (p@ss5678). (Note, each of the following commands should be entered on a single line.):

   ```
   ciscoasa(config)# aaa-server RADIUSSERVERS protocol radius
   ciscoasa(config-aaa-server-group)# aaa-server RADIUSSERVERS (inside) host 192.168.1.15
   ```

   (where 192.168.1.15 is the IP address of the RADIUS server)

   ```
   ciscoasa(config-aaa-server-host)# key p@ss5678
   ciscoasa(config-aaa-server-host)# exit
   ```

3. While still in global configuration mode, specify the services you wish to have authenticated through RADIUS, making sure to include local authentication as a backup in case the authentication server is not available:

```
ciscoasa(config)# aaa authentication ssh console RADIUSSERVERS LOCAL
```

```
ciscoasa(config)#
ciscoasa(config)# aaa-server RADIUSSERVERS protocol radius
ciscoasa(config-aaa-server-group)# aaa-server RADIUSSERVERS (inside) host 192.168.1.15
ciscoasa(config-aaa-server-host)# key p@ss5678
ciscoasa(config-aaa-server-host)# exit
ciscoasa(config)# aaa authentication ssh console RADIUSSERVERS LOCAL
ciscoasa(config)#
```

Figure 100: Configuring an ASA for RADIUS authentication

4. If you receive an error in entering the above commands, check to be sure that aaa authentication is not already configured with the following command:

```
ciscoasa# show run aaa
```

5. You should see output similar to this (it may not be exactly what you see below):

```
aaa authentication ssh console LOCAL

aaa authentication enable console LOCAL

aaa authentication telnet console LOCAL

aaa authorization command LOCAL
```

6. If aaa authentication is already configured (perhaps from a previous exercise), you must first remove it before configuring aaa authentication through RADIUS. In the Cisco command-line, you can remove configuration statements by preceding the same statement used to enable a configuration with the modifier "no". For example, you can remove the previous aaa ssh configuration with this command:

```
ciscoasa(config)# no aaa authentication ssh console LOCAL
```

7. When you have completed the configuration, log off the firewall and, using SSH, attempt to re-login as *user01* with a password of *p@ss1234*. Your login should be successful.

CHAPTER 6:
Configuring the Appliance as a DHCP Server

"Computers are incredibly fast, accurate and stupid. Humans beings are incredibly slow, inaccurate and brilliant. Together they are powerful beyond imagination."

--Albert Einstein

Configuring DHCP on an ASA Security Appliance

The Cisco security appliance can provide Dynamic Host Configuration Protocol (DHCP) services to your network. A DHCP server can be configured on each virtual (VLAN) interface of the appliance. A unique pool of addresses can be configured on each of the interfaces, but DHCP options such as DNS servers and domain names, default gateways, etc. are configured globally and apply to all interfaces.

The Cisco ASA is not a very versatile DHCP server, compared to a Windows or Linux server or even compared to a Cisco router. For example, it does not support the configuration of DHCP reservations, but it is adequate for use in a small office/home office environment.

Hands-On Exercise 6.1:
Reconfiguring Your DHCP Server

In the real world, you might just decide to use default settings for your inside network, which means you won't need to reconfigure your DHCP server. That means you'll use the inside network of 192.168.1.0/24 and you don't need to make any changes. If, however, you want to use a different network address and the appliance's DHCP server, you'll also need to modify the scope of addresses and other parameters in the DHCP server.

In this exercise, you will use the CLI to reconfigure your firewall's internal IP address and its DHCP address pool.

Exercise Diagram

For this exercise, you will start with the same network configuration as that used in earlier chapters. You will, however, modify the configuration to support a different IP address on the inside interface and a different DHCP pool from the default.

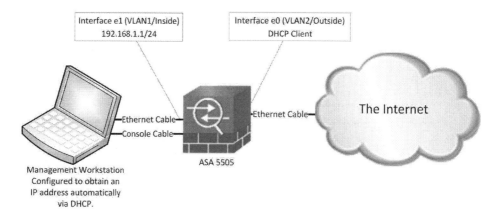

Figure 101: DHCP exercise starting configuration

Exercise Prerequisites

This exercise assumes that you performed the steps in the previous chapter to create a user with the username of user15 and that user15 has full administrative privileges on the security appliance.

Exercise Steps

Assign a Different IP Address to Your Inside Interface

For the purpose of this exercise, you'll use the following settings in your DHCP server configuration:

- Inside interface address: 192.168.101.1

- Inside interface subnet mask: 255.255.255.0

- DHCP address range: 192.168.101.6-192.168.101.37

- DNS servers: 8.8.8.8 8.8.4.4 (these are the Google public DNS servers)

- Domain name: soundtraining.net

Of course, feel free to modify these with your own settings. It's easier, however, when you're first learning, to just use the same settings as me.

1. Log in as user15 with the password p@ss1234.

2. Assign a new IP address for your firewall's inside interface using the following commands:

   ```
   ciscoasa# conf t
   ciscoasa(config)# interface vlan1
   ciscoasa(config-if)# ip address 192.168.101.1
   ```

3. Notice that the change causes the device to display a warning due to a conflict with your DHCP address pool.

```
asa01(config)# int vlan 1
asa01(config-if)# ip address 192.168.101.1
Interface address is not on same subnet as DHCP pool
WARNING: DHCPD bindings cleared on interface 'inside', address pool removed
asa01(config-if)#
```

Figure 102: Changing an IP address on the inside interface

If You're Running an Earlier Version of the ASA Software

In earlier versions (prior to 9.0(4)) of the ASA software, the change actually fails and in order to make these changes, you must first remove the existing DHCP scope. The easiest way to do so is by showing the current scope with the following command:

```
ciscoasa(config)# show run dhcpd
```

You'll see a line similar to this:

```
dhcpd address 192.168.1.6-192.168.1.30 inside
```

Use your mouse to capture (copy) the line. In your firewall's command-line interface, enter the word "no", followed by a space, then paste the above line into the CLI so that it looks similar to this:

```
ciscoasa(config)# no dhcpd address 192.168.1.6-192.168.1.37 inside
```

(Note: If the above command fails, check the actual dhcp configuration on your firewall with the show run dhcpd command. You may need to adjust the starting and ending addresses in the pool to match your firewall's actual configuration.)

You should now be able to change your firewall's internal IP address with the following commands. Notice that the firewall does not require you to enter a subnet mask. It automatically appends the default mask based on the class of address.

```
ciscoasa(config)# interface vlan1
ciscoasa(config-if)# ip address 192.168.101.1
```

In version 9.0(4) and later the software will remove the DHCPD bindings for you.

Configure a New DHCP Pool

4. Configure a new DHCP pool for clients on your inside interface with the following command:

```
ciscoasa(config-if)# dhcpd address 192.168.101.5-192.168.101.37 inside
```

5. Add a default route (also known as a "default gateway" or a "gateway of last resort" using DHCP option 3 (the standard DHCP option number for the default router)

```
ciscoasa(config)# dhcpd option 3 ip 192.168.101.1
```

6. Configure DNS servers for your DHCP clients:

```
ciscoasa(config)# dhcpd dns 8.8.8.8 8.8.4.4
```

7. Configure a DNS domain name for your DHCP clients (of course, you can change this to whatever you wish; it's just a default domain name if none is supplied by the client):

```
ciscoasa(config)# dhcpd domain soundtraining.net
```

8. Enable the new pool with the following command:

```
ciscoasa(config)# dhcpd enable inside
```

```
ciscoasa#
ciscoasa# conf t
ciscoasa(config)# interface vlan1
ciscoasa(config-if)# ip address 192.168.101.1
Interface address is not on same subnet as DHCP pool
WARNING: DHCPD bindings cleared on interface 'inside', address pool removed
Waiting for the earlier webvpn instance to terminate...
Previous instance shut down. Starting a new one.
ciscoasa(config-if)# dhcpd address 192.168.101.5-192.168.101.37 inside
ciscoasa(config)# dhcpd option 3 ip 192.168.101.1
ciscoasa(config)# dhcpd dns 8.8.8.8 8.8.4.4
ciscoasa(config)# dhcpd domain soundtraining.net
ciscoasa(config)# dhcpd enable inside
ciscoasa(config)#
```

Figure 103: DHCP server configuration commands

9. In the command-line interface of your management workstation, release and renew your computer's IP address.

ipconfig /release

ipconfig /renew

You should immediately see a new IP address from the newly configured pool.

Now that you have made additional changes to your configuration, save it to flash memory and back it up to your TFTP server using the procedures you learned earlier:

```
ciscoasa(config)# wr
```

```
ciscoasa(config)# copy run tftp://192.168.101.5/config_dhcpd.txt
```

(**Note:** You may need to change the above IP address to the one assigned to your management workstation if it's different from the one I'm using. It's also possible that you might need to restart your TFTP server before this command will work.)

CHAPTER 7:
Access Control Lists

"In the end, like most other things having to do with systems engineering it's not about finding the right way, but about finding the best-possible-under-the-circumstances way of doing things."

—Tres Wong-Godfrey

Understanding Access Control Lists

Access Control Lists (ACLs) are lists of permit and deny conditions applied to traffic flows and based on various criteria including protocol type source IP address, destination IP address, source port number, and/or destination port number.

ACLs can be used to filter traffic for various purposes including security, monitoring, route selection, and network address translation. ACLs are comprised of one or more Access Control Entries (ACEs). Each ACE is an individual line within an ACL.

Watch the Video

There is a video on my YouTube channel in which I demonstrate the following procedures. Watch the video at http://youtu.be/w2Gz0yOgZkg.

Rules for Access-Control Lists

- Packets are evaluated against entries in an ACL in sequential order.

- Once a packet matches an entry, no further evaluation is done.

- There is an implicit "deny any" at the end of every ACL, so any packet not explicitly permitted is implicitly denied. In other words, if a packet does not match any entry in an ACL, that packet is dropped.

Types of Access-Control Lists

There are fundamentally two types of access-control lists: standard ACLs and extended ACLs.

Standard ACLs filter based only on the source IP address of a packet.

Extended ACLs filter based on the source and/or destination IP address, protocol type such as IP, TCP, UDP, ICMP, and others, and source and/or destination TCP/UDP port numbers.

Soundthinking Point:
Order of Entries in an
ACL is Important

When building ACLs, put entries in order from most specific to most general.

ACL Syntax

ACLs on a Cisco ASA Security Appliance are similar to those on a Cisco router, but not identical. Firewalls use real subnet masks instead of the inverse mask (wildcard bits) used on a router. ACLs on a firewall are named instead of numbered and assumed to be an extended list.

The syntax of an ACE is relatively straight-forward:

```
ciscoasa(config)#access-list name [line number] [extended] {permit | deny}
protocol source _ IP _ address source _ netmask [operator source _ port]
destination _ IP _ address destination _ netmask [operator destination _ port]
[log [[disable | default] | [level]] [interval seconds]] [time-range name]
[inactive]
```

```
ciscoasa(config)# access-list demo1 permit tcp 10.1.0.0 255.255.255.0 any eq www
ciscoasa(config)# access-list demo1 permit tcp 10.1.0.0 255.255.255.0 any eq 443
ciscoasa(config)# show access-list
access-list cached ACL log flows: total 0, denied 0 (deny-flow-max 4096)
            alert-interval 300
access-list demo1; 2 elements; name hash: 0x9fef7141
access-list demo1 line 1 extended permit tcp 10.1.0.0 255.255.255.0 any eq www (hitcnt=0) 0x3f8412a5
access-list demo1 line 2 extended permit tcp 10.1.0.0 255.255.255.0 any eq https (hitcnt=0) 0xf420b1e8
ciscoasa(config)#
```

Figure 104: Creating an access control list (ACL)

In the above example, an ACL called "demo1" is created in which the first ACE permits TCP traffic originating on the 10.1.0.0 subnet to go to any destination IP address with the destination port of 80 (www). In the second ACE, the same traffic flow is permitted for destination port 443. Notice in the output of the *show access-list* that line numbers are displayed and the *extended* parameter is also included, even though neither was included in the configuration statements.

You can deactivate an ACE without deleting it by appending the *inactive* option to the end of the line.

As with Cisco routers, there is an implicit "deny any" at the end of every ACL. Any traffic that is not explicitly permitted is implicitly denied.

Editing ACLs and ACEs

New ACEs are appended to the end of the ACL. If you want, however, to insert the new ACE at a particular location within the ACL, you can add the line number parameter to the ACE:

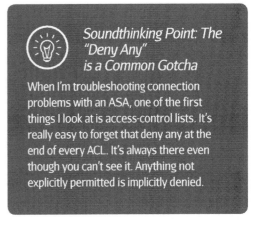

Soundthinking Point: The "Deny Any" is a Common Gotcha

When I'm troubleshooting connection problems with an ASA, one of the first things I look at is access-control lists. It's really easy to forget that deny any at the end of every ACL. It's always there even though you can't see it. Anything not explicitly permitted is implicitly denied.

```
ciscoasa(config)# show access-list demo1
access-list demo1; 2 elements; name hash: 0x9fef7141
access-list demo1 line 1 extended permit tcp 10.1.0.0 255.255.255.0 any eq www (hitcnt=0) 0x3f8412a5
access-list demo1 line 2 extended permit tcp 10.1.0.0 255.255.255.0 any eq https (hitcnt=0) 0xf420b1e8
ciscoasa(config)# access-list demo1 line 2 deny tcp host 10.1.0.2 any eq https
ciscoasa(config)# show access-list demo1
access-list demo1; 3 elements; name hash: 0x9fef7141
access-list demo1 line 1 extended permit tcp 10.1.0.0 255.255.255.0 any eq www (hitcnt=0) 0x3f8412a5
access-list demo1 line 2 extended deny tcp host 10.1.0.2 any eq https (hitcnt=0) 0xdae95b55
access-list demo1 line 3 extended permit tcp 10.1.0.0 255.255.255.0 any eq https (hitcnt=0) 0xf420b1e8
ciscoasa(config)#
```

Figure 105: Editing an access control list

Notice in the fifth line of the example above that an ACE is added at line two in the ACL. Notice in the output from the *show access-list demo1* command that the new entry is added in the second position in the ACL and the former second entry becomes line number three.

You can remove an ACE from an ACL by preceding the ACE configuration statement with the modifier *no*, as in the following example:

```
ciscoasa(config)#
ciscoasa(config)# no access-list demo1 deny tcp host 10.1.0.2 any eq https
ciscoasa(config)#
```

Figure 106: Removing an entry from an ACL

Time ranges can be used with ACEs to enable the ACE during specific time parameters. Configuring time ranges is a two-part process. Part one is naming and creating the time range. Part two is configuring the ACE with the time range.

Time-ranges permit the use of either periodic ranges, such as every week day, or absolute ranges, such as February 1 through February 14. Use the following syntax for naming and creating the time-range:

Periodic

ciscoasa(config)#**time-range name**

ciscoasa(config-time-range)#**periodic days-of-the-week time to time**

Absolute

ciscoasa(config)#**time-range name**

ciscoasa(config-time-range)#**absolute start time date [end time date]**

The time is expressed in 24:00 time and the date is expressed in day, month, year.

```
ciscoasa(config)#
ciscoasa(config)# time-range workweek
ciscoasa(config-time-range)# periodic weekdays 08:00 to 17:00
ciscoasa(config-time-range)# access-list www_restrict deny tcp any any eq www time-range workweek
ciscoasa(config)#
```

Figure 107: Configuring a time-range

ACLs can be renamed with the following simple command:

```
ciscoasa(config)#
ciscoasa(config)# access-list www_restrict rename web_restrict
ciscoasa(config)#
```

Figure 108:
Renaming an access-list

In the above example, the ACL *www_restrict* is renamed to *web_restrict*.

Object Groups

Object Groups simplify ACL management by grouping similar components together for inclusion in an ACE. There are five types of object groups available on the ASA Security Appliance:

- Network object group: One or more IP addresses

- Protocol object group: One or more IP protocols

- ICMP object group: One or more ICMP types

- Basic service object group: One or more TCP or UDP port numbers

- Enhanced service object group: Mix of protocols, ICMP types, UDP/TCP ports

In the following example, a network object group is created with the name *Accounting*. Note the use of the description command to document the object group's purpose. This particular object group identifies a single host at 10.1.0.1 and the subnet 10.2.0.0/24.

Figure 109:
Configuring an
object group

```
ciscoasa(config)#
ciscoasa(config)# object-group network Accounting
ciscoasa(config-network-object-group)# description Accounting and Finance
ciscoasa(config-network-object-group)# network-object host 10.1.0.1
ciscoasa(config-network-object-group)# network-object 10.2.0.0 255.255.255.0
ciscoasa(config-network-object-group)# exit
ciscoasa(config)# _
```

The object group can be applied to an ACE as follows:

```
ciscoasa(config)#
ciscoasa(config)# access-list demo2 permit tcp object-group Accounting any eq www
ciscoasa(config)# access-list demo2 permit tcp object-group Accounting any eq 443
ciscoasa(config)#
```

Figure 110: Using an object group in an access-list

Notice how the ACL demo2 permits hosts identified in the object-group *Accounting* to access port 80 and 443 on any host.

Using Access-Control Lists

In order for an ACL to have any effect, it must be applied to an interface or a function. In the following example, the ACL is designed to permit inside hosts to ping hosts on an outside network such as the public Internet. In the example shown, "101" is just a label for the list. It could just as easily be a descriptive name such as "permit_ping". (ICMP stands for Internet Control Message Protocol, the protocol used by ping and some other network utilities.)

The first four lines in the example identify and permit the traffic flows. The last line applies the list to inbound traffic on the outside interface. Note the use of the "access-group 101" statement which applies access-list 101 to the interface.

```
access-list 101 permit icmp any any echo-reply

access-list 101 permit icmp any any source-quench

access-list 101 permit icmp any any unreachable

access-list 101 permit icmp any any time-exceeded

access-group 101 in interface outside
```

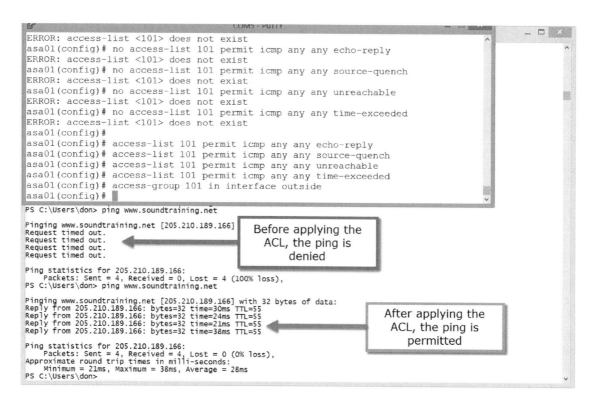

Figure 111: How to permit ping packets through the firewall

The above access-control list permits several types of ICMP traffic in addition to ping packets. If you want to allow only ping packets, use the following commands:

```
access-list 101 permit icmp any any echo-reply

access-group 101 in interface outside
```

Understanding Network Address Translation (NAT)

NAT is the process of substituting one address for another or having one address represent many addresses. Two common forms of NAT are static NAT and Port Address Translation.

Static NAT maps one address to another such as when an Internet-accessible server is located behind a firewall. In that case, Internet users would use an outside address on the firewall to connect to the internal server. The firewall would translate the incoming request and forward the request to the server's inside address.

Port Address Translation is a many-to-one mapping such as used on home networks where a single public address on the Internet is shared by multiple internal hosts using private space RFC 1918 (http://www.rfc-editor.org/rfc/rfc1918.txt) addresses.

Understanding NAT Terminology

Real address

The real address is the address that is configured on a host, before translation. Real addresses can be on inside or outside networks. Think of real addresses as non-translated addresses. The real address is often on the inside network and, frankly, it's also usually an RFC 1918 address.

Mapped address

A mapped address is what the real address is translated to. The mapped address is usually the address on the security appliance's outside interface, but that's certainly not a requirement.

Bidirectional initiation

As opposed to Port Address Translation, Static NAT allows connections to be initiated in either direction, both to and from the host.

NAT Implementations

Cisco ASA security appliances implement NAT either through Network Object NAT or Twice NAT.

Network Object NAT

Network Objects are simply a means of grouping IP address-related components such as subnets and/or individual hosts. You can use Network Objects in many places in the appliances configuration including NAT, access rules, or even in Twice NAT configurations.

Twice NAT

Twice NAT uses a single rule to match both the source and destination address.

Network Object NAT is easier to use and more reliable, especially with applications such as VoIP. Twice NAT provides greater granularity of configuration. For the purpose of this book, I will focus on Network Object NAT.

Configuring Network Object NAT

Three steps are involved in configuring Network Object NAT:

1. Create the object

2. Populate the object with IP address information

3. Create the NAT statement

Configuring Port Address Translation

For example, to configure port address translation (PAT) in which the 192.168.1.0/24 subnet, connected to the inside interface, is protected behind the address on the outside interface, you would enter the following three statements in global configuration mode:

ciscoasa(config)#**object network net-192.168.1**

ciscoasa(config-network-object)#**subnet 192.168.1.0 255.255.255.0**

ciscoasa(config-network-object)#**nat (inside,outside) dynamic interface**

```
ciscoasa(config)# object network net-192.168.1
ciscoasa(config-network-object)# subnet 192.168.1.0 255.255.255.0
ciscoasa(config-network-object)# nat (inside,outside) dynamic interface
ciscoasa(config-network-object)#
```

Figure 112: Configuring Port Address Translation

Configuring Static NAT

To configure static NAT in which inbound TCP port 80 requests on the outside interface are forwarded to an internal webserver located at 192.168.1.2, you would enter the following three statements in global configuration mode:

ciscoasa(config)#**object network www-host**

ciscoasa(config-network-object)#**host 192.168.1.2**

ciscoasa(config-network-object)#**nat (inside,outside) static interface service tcp www www**

In the above configuration, the first line creates the network object and names it www-host, the second line specifies the location of the Web server that is the destination of the HTTP packets, and the third line does the actual mapping. In the third line, the nat statement implements network address translation, the (*inside,outside*) statement specifies the real and the mapped interfaces, *static* specifies the type of NAT (as opposed to *dynamic*), *interface* tells NAT to use whatever IP address is on the outside interface as the mapped address, *service* tells NAT to use port mapping, *tcp* tells NAT to use TCP as the transport protocol (as opposed to UDP), the first *www* is the real TCP port (80), and the second *www* is the mapped TCP port (80).

```
ciscoasa(config)#
ciscoasa(config)# object network www-host
ciscoasa(config-network-object)# host 192.168.1.2
ciscoasa(config-network-object)# nat (inside,outside) static interface service tcp www www
ciscoasa(config-network-object)#
```

Figure 113: Configuring static NAT

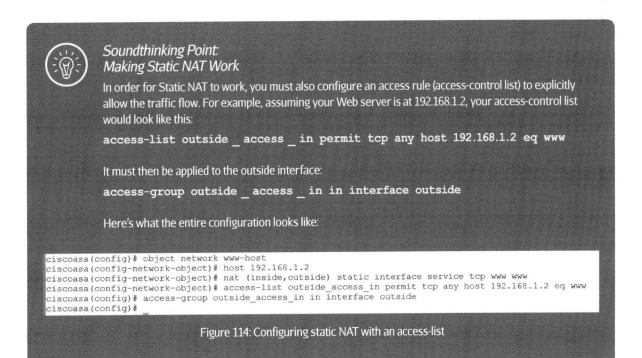

Soundthinking Point:
Making Static NAT Work

In order for Static NAT to work, you must also configure an access rule (access-control list) to explicitly allow the traffic flow. For example, assuming your Web server is at 192.168.1.2, your access-control list would look like this:

```
access-list outside _ access _ in permit tcp any host 192.168.1.2 eq www
```

It must then be applied to the outside interface:

```
access-group outside _ access _ in in interface outside
```

Here's what the entire configuration looks like:

```
ciscoasa(config)# object network www-host
ciscoasa(config-network-object)# host 192.168.1.2
ciscoasa(config-network-object)# nat (inside,outside) static interface service tcp www www
ciscoasa(config-network-object)# access-list outside_access_in permit tcp any host 192.168.1.2 eq www
ciscoasa(config)# access-group outside_access_in in interface outside
ciscoasa(config)#
```

Figure 114: Configuring static NAT with an access-list

CHAPTER 8:
Virtual Private Networking (VPNs)

"1f u c4n r34d th1s u r34lly r 4 g33k."

—Unknown

Understanding the Purpose and Types of Virtual Private Networks

Virtual Private Networking (VPN) allows corporate users working remotely to connect securely to the corporate LAN across a non-secure network such as the public Internet. A physical connection is first established between the remote user and the corporate network, then a VPN tunnel is established which encrypts traffic between the remote user and the corporate network. VPNs allow companies to support remote connections without the expense of dedicated leased lines or the poor performance of dial-up service.

VPNs can be divided into two broad categories: Site-to-site VPNs and remote access VPNs.

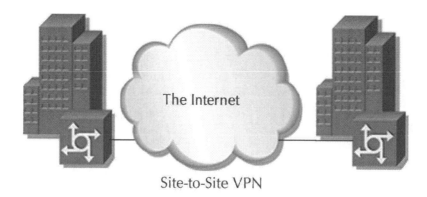

Site-to-Site VPN

Figure 114: A site-to-site (or lan-to-lan) VPN in which the boxes with arrows represent firewalls connecting two office buildings to the Internet

Site-to-site VPNs are used to connect branch offices to a corporate LAN, for vendors and suppliers to connect to a corporate LAN, and for customers who need an "always-on" connection to a corporate LAN.

Such VPNs are often used as replacements for expensive, dedicated services such as T1 lines between offices.

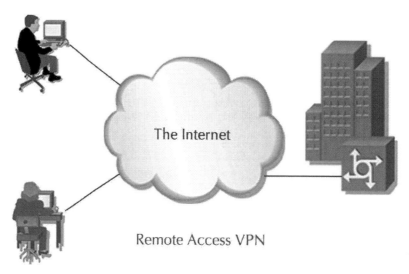

Remote Access VPN

Figure 115: A remote access VPN

Remote access VPNs are used by mobile workers who need to connect to the corporate LAN while on the road or working temporarily from a remote location.

VPN Protocols

PPTP

PPTP is Point-to-Point Tunneling Protocol. PPTP is a legacy VPN protocol based on RFC 2637, which was published in 1999. PPTP is widely supported, but is generally considered less robust than L2TP. Although most desktop and handheld operating systems include a PPTP client, PPTP is not supported in the Cisco ASA Security Appliance. PPTP is generally considered to be a non-secure protocol and should not normally be used in a production environment.

L2TP

L2TP is Layer Two Tunneling Protocol. Developed by Cisco Systems, L2TP is based on PPTP and includes some of the features of PPTP. L2TP is generally regarded as a more robust VPN solution than PPTP. In addition to being supported by most desktop and handheld operating systems, L2TP is also supported for remote access connections in the Cisco ASA Security Appliance.

IPSec VPN

IPSec (Internet Protocol Security) is a framework of open-standard protocols that combine to provide authentication, integrity, and confidentiality. IPSec operates at layer three of the OSI model. It uses Internet Key Exchange (IKE) to establish a security association (SA) between two peers. In an IPSec VPN connection, two phases of negotiation take place. Phase one is the key exchange using IKE that establishes a security association. As soon as the IKE SA is established, phase two negotiations begin which are used to establish the IPSec SA. The IPSec SA is used to create unidirectional security associations between two IPSec peers.

Phase One Negotiations

Think of phase one as being the introduction and handshake in the process of creating a VPN connection. During phase one negotiation, the peers determine the encryption algorithm, the hash algorithm, and the authentication method, and the Diffie-Hellman group.

Encryption Algorithms

- **DES (Data Encryption Standard)** DES is a 56-bit encryption algorithm which is not generally considered secure for sensitive communications.

- **3DES (Triple Data Encryption Standard)** 3DES provides 168-bit encryption by using DES to encrypt the data three times consecutively. In 3DES, the data is first encrypted with a DES key, then decrypted with a second DES key, and finally encrypted with a third DES key.

- **AES (Advanced Encryption Standard)** AES is based on the Rijndael algorithm which encrypts and decrypts the data with cryptographic keys that are 128, 192, or 256 bits long.

Hashing Algorithms

A hashing algorithm takes input in the form of a message and outputs a fixed-length message digest. The message digest is incorporated into the digital signature algorithm. The digital signature algorithm is used to generate or verify the message's signature.

Cisco Security Appliances support HMAC (Keyed-Hash Message Authentication Code) variants of these common hashing algorithms:

- **SHA-1 (Secure Hash Algorithm)** SHA-1 outputs a 160-bit digest.

- **MD5 (Message Digest 5)** MD5 outputs a 128-bit digest

SHA-1's 160-bit digest is considered more secure than MD5's 128-bit digest, but MD5 is slightly faster due to its smaller digest.

Authentication Method

Cisco security appliances support two methods for authenticating IPSec peers:

- **RSA Signatures:** RSA signatures are based on a PKI using digital certificates authenticated by RSA signatures.

- **Preshared Keys:** A preshared key is a password. It is a case-sensitive value entered manually into each peer which authenticates the peer.

Diffie-Hellman Group

Diffie-Hellman is a PKI protocol used by two IPSec peers to produce a shared secret across non-secure channels without transmitting it to each other. Cisco Security Appliances support three Diffie-Hellman groups: Group 1 is 768 bits, group 2 is 1024 bits, and group 3 is 1536 bits.

Phase Two Negotiations

Think of phase two of creating the VPN as the phase where the peers actually create a secure tunnel.

The negotiations that take place in phase two are used to establish unidirectional security associations between the two IPSec peers. The algorithms, protocols, and keying used between the peers are determined by the SAs.

The two primary security protocols supported by the Cisco security appliance and used in IPSec communications are:

ESP (Encapsulating Security Payload) IANA protocol number 50, ESP provides services in the areas of authentication, encryption, and antireplay. ESP can be used to encrypt the entire packet or just the data payload.

AH (Authentication Header) IANA protocol number 51, AH does not provide encryption service, but does provide data authentication and anti-replay. AH cannot be used with NAT because it provides only origin authentication or verification that the data is actually from the sender. When NAT is used, the translation occurs before the security association is established which changes the source address. That, in turn, causes the hashing process to fail.

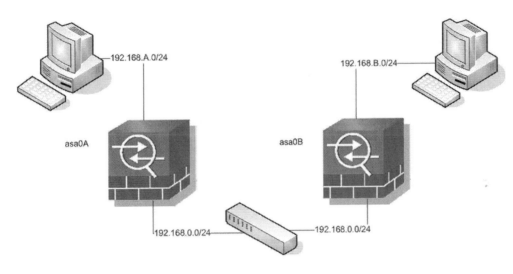

Figure 116: A site-to-site (l2l or lan2lan) VPN

Hands-On Exercise 8.1:
Configuring Site-to-Site VPNs Using the Command Line Interface

In this exercise, you will simulate a VPN connecting two geographically separate offices across the public Internet. Each security appliance can function as both initiator and/or responder. This exercise will be completed using the Command Line Interface (CLI).

You will peer one ASA appliance with a second ASA appliance to complete this exercise.

Exercise Diagram

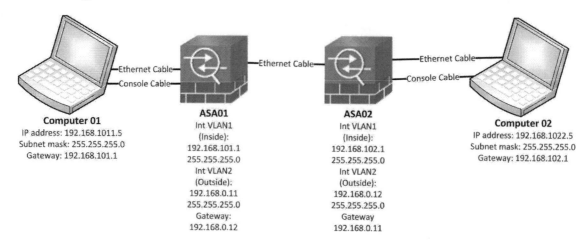

Figure 117: Network diagram for the site-to-site VPN exercise

Exercise Prerequisites

Two Cisco ASA Security Appliances, running software version 9.x. The exercise is written using two 5505s, but should work with any two ASAs. The procedures are similar for earlier software versions as far back as 8.3, but may require slight adjustments.

Two computers, each equipped with an Ethernet adapter and configured with a static IP address as indicated in the exercise diagram.

Watch the Video

There is a video on my YouTube channel in which I demonstrate the following procedures. Watch the video at http://youtu.be/sIbi_bYb2k4.

Exercise Steps

Save the Appliance's Current Running Configuration to Flash Memory

Enter the following command to save your current configuration to flash memory:

asa#**write mem** (You can abbreviate this as simply **wr**.)

IMPORTANT: Do not save your configuration to flash memory again during the VPN exercises. After the VPN exercises, you will reload your ASA to return to a pristine configuration.

Attempt the Remote Connection

Note: In order for this exercise to work, you must either allow ICMP through the Windows firewall or disable the firewall. In a real world setting, you should not normally disable the Windows firewall or other host-based firewalls. The procedure to manage the Windows firewall varies based on your operating system. In Windows 7 or 8, go to your Control Panel, then System and Security, then Windows Firewall.

1. On each computer, disable the Windows firewall to ensure that the computer will respond to a ping. Test it by attempting to ping the paired computer from the ASA security appliance. In other words, attempt to ping Computer 01 from ASA01 and attempt to ping Computer 02 from ASA02. If this ping is not successful, troubleshoot by ensuring that cables are properly connected and Windows firewalls are disabled or otherwise configured to permit ICMP traffic.

2. On each computer, start a continuous ping to the remote host (the other computer):

   a. Click on Start, then click on Run (or use the key combination of Win+R).

   b. In the Run dialog window, enter "cmd" to open a command window.

3. From Computer 01, start a continuous ping to Computer 02 with the following command:

   `ping -t 192.168.102.5` (The option -t makes the ping continuous until disabled with the key combination of ctrl+c.)

4. From Computer 02, start a continuous ping to Computer 01 with the following command:

   `ping -t 192.168.101.5`

5. Notice that neither ping is successful at this time. Leave the pings running.

6. Move the command window to the edge of your screen where it will be visible while you configure your appliance and leave the ping running.

Building the Tunnel

7. Enter *global configuration mode*

   ```
   ciscoasa# config t
   ```

8. Enable ISAKMP on the outside interface

   ```
   ciscoasa(config)# crypto isakmp enable outside
   ```

Create the Network Objects

Network objects are simply a way of identifying individual hosts or groups of hosts on a network. They can be reused in various configurations.

ASA	Inside Subnet and Mask	Outside Interface Address
asa01	192.168.101.0 255.255.255.0	192.168.0.11
asa02	192.168.102.0 255.255.255.0	192.168.0.12

9. Create a network object for your inside subnet. Refer to the above table or the exercise diagram for your inside subnet address and mask.

   ciscoasa(config)# **object network net-local**

   ciscoasa(config-network-object)# **subnet [YOUR INSIDE SUBNET & MASK]**

10. Create a network object for the remote subnet on the other security appliance.

    ciscoasa(config-network-object)# **object network net-remote**

    ciscoasa(config-network-object)# **subnet [THE OTHER ASA'S INSIDE SUBNET AND MASK]**

    ciscoasa(config-network-object)# **exit**

Create an Access-Control List

11. Create an access-control list to identify the traffic flow from your inside subnet to the remote inside subnet:

    ciscoasa(config)# **access-list outside _ 1 _ cryptomap permit ip object net-local object net-remote**

```
asa01(config)#
asa01(config)# crypto isakmp enable outside
asa01(config)# object network net-local
asa01(config-network-object)# subnet 192.168.101.0 255.255.255.0
asa01(config-network-object)# object network net-remote
asa01(config-network-object)# subnet 192.168.102.0 255.255.255.0
asa01(config-network-object)# exit
asa01(config)# access-list outside_1_cryptomap permit ip object net-local object net-remote
asa01(config)#
```

Figure 118: Configuring and applying access-lists for a one side of a site-to-site VPN

138

Create and Configure the Tunnel Group

12. Create a tunnel-group to identify the remote firewall's outside interface and the type of VPN (ipsec, lan-to-lan):

    ciscoasa(config)# **tunnel-group [OTHER ASA'S OUTSIDE IP ADDRESS] type ipsec-l2l**

    (Note: l2l is the letter "l" as in lan-2-lan, not the number "one".)

13. Create a tunnel-group to set tunnel attributes including the shared key and keepalives:

    ciscoasa(config)# **tunnel-group [OTHER ASA'S OUTSIDE IP ADDRESS] ipsec-attributes**

    ciscoasa(config-tunnel-ipsec)# **pre-shared-key p@ss5678**

    ciscoasa(config-tunnel-ipsec)# **isakmp keepalive threshold 10 retry 2**

    ciscoasa(config-tunnel-ipsec)# **exit**

```
asa01(config)#
asa01(config)# tunnel-group 192.168.0.12 type ipsec-l2l
asa01(config)# tunnel-group 192.168.0.12 ipsec-attributes
asa01(config-tunnel-ipsec)# pre-shared-key p@ss5678
asa01(config-tunnel-ipsec)# isakmp keepalive threshold 10 retry 2
asa01(config-tunnel-ipsec)# exit
asa01(config)# ▉
```

Figure 119:
Configuring the tunnel
group for one side of
a site-to-site VPN

Configure Phase 1

Phase one is where the two firewalls handshake to manage the key exchange. This portion of the configuration uses asynchronous key cryptography.

14. Create an isakmp policy to specify the authentication method

    ciscoasa(config)# **crypto isakmp policy 10 authentication pre-share**

15. Create an isakmp policy to specify the encryption algorithm

    ciscoasa(config)# **crypto isakmp policy 10 encrypt aes**

16. Create an isakmp policy to specify the hashing algorithm

    ciscoasa(config)# **crypto isakmp policy 10 hash sha**

17. Create an isakmp policy to specify the Diffie-Hellman group

    ciscoasa(config)# **crypto isakmp policy 10 group 2**

18. Create an isakmp policy to specify the key lifetime

    ciscoasa(config)# **crypto isakmp policy 10 lifetime 86400**

```
asa01(config)#
asa01(config)# crypto isakmp policy 10 authentication pre-share
asa01(config)# crypto isakmp policy 10 encrypt aes
asa01(config)# crypto isakmp policy 10 hash sha
asa01(config)# crypto isakmp policy 10 group 2
asa01(config)# crypto isakmp policy 10 lifetime 86400
asa01(config)# _
```

Figure 120:
Configuring phase
one settings for
a site-to-site VPN

Configure Phase 2

Phase two is the configuration used for the actual tunnel. It is based on synchronous key cryptography.

19. Create an ipsec policy to specify the encryption and hashing algorithms to be used on the tunnel:

    ciscoasa(config)# **crypto ipsec transform-set ESP-AES-SHA esp-aes esp-sha-hmac**

20. Create a crypto map entry to identify an already configured access-control list that identifies the traffic flow(s) to be protected

    ciscoasa(config)# **crypto map outside _ map 1 match address outside _ 1 _ cryptomap**

21. Create a crypto map entry to enable perfect forward secrecy using Diffie-Hellman group 2. (PFS periodically generates new session keys for encrypted messages, thus making it more difficult for an attacker to use captured keys to decrypt a message.)

    ciscoasa(config)# **crypto map outside _ map 1 set pfs group2**

22. Create a crypto map entry to identify the remote firewall's outside interface IP address:

    ciscoasa(config)# **crypto map outside _ map 1 set peer [OTHER ASA'S OUTSIDE IP ADDRESS]**

23. Create a crypto map entry to identify the transform-set which will be applied to the tunnel

    ciscoasa(config)# **crypto map outside _ map 1 set transform-set ESP-AES-SHA**

24. Apply the crypto map to the outside interface

```
ciscoasa(config)# crypto map outside _ map interface outside
```

```
asa01(config)# crypto ipsec transform-set ESP-AES-SHA esp-aes esp-sha-hmac
asa01(config)# crypto map outside_map 1 match address outside_1_cryptomap
asa01(config)# crypto map outside_map 1 set pfs group2
asa01(config)# crypto map outside_map 1 set  peer 192.168.0.12
asa01(config)# crypto map outside_map 1 set  transform-set  ESP-AES-SHA
asa01(config)# crypto map outside_map interface outside
asa01(config)#
```

Figure 121: Phase two configuration on one of the hosts for a site-to-site VPN

Configure NAT

25. Create a NAT statement to prevent tunnel traffic from being NAT'ed (that's the number 1, not the letter "l").

```
ciscoasa(config)# nat (inside,outside) 1 source static net-local net-local
destination static net-remote net-remote
```

Configure a Default Route

1. Create a default route:

   On ASA01, use the following command:

   ```
   ciscoasa(config)# route outside 0 0 192.168.0.12
   ```

   On ASA02, use the following command:

   ```
   ciscoasa(config)# route outside 0 0 192.168.0.11
   ```

```
asa01(config)# nat (inside,outside) 1 source static net-local net-local destination static net-rem
ote net-remote
asa01(config)# route outside 0 0 192.168.0.12
asa01(config)#
```

Figure 122: Site-to-site VPN configuration of NAT and default rroute

(In the real world, the default route is probably provided by your ISP.)

When you have correctly completed the above steps, the ping should now be successful. If it is not, check for spelling and typographical errors. Additionally, look in the next section for troubleshooting tools.

Upon completion of this exercise, be sure to re-enable the Windows firewall on each computer where you previously disabled it.

Troubleshooting VPN Connections

As with most Cisco products, the show and debug commands are very helpful in both understanding and troubleshooting VPN connections.

To review your configuration, use the following commands and compare the output of each command to the steps in the exercise:

- `show run crypto`
- `show run object`
- `show run access-list`

- `show run tunnel-group`
- `show run nat`
- `show run route`

`show crypto protocol statistics all` will display a summary of security protocol statistics on your security appliance.

`show isakmp` will display ISAKMP operational data including active and previous tunnels, plus the number and type of ISAKMP requests and responses.

`show isakmp stats` will display more detailed ISAKMP operational data.

`show isakmp sa` will display ISAKMP security associations. If there are no isakmp sas, then there can't be any ipsec activity.

`show ipsec sa` will display IPSec security associations.

`show ipsec stats` will display IPSec global statistics including active and previous tunnels.

`debug crypto isakmp 7` will show the IKE setup process. (The number "7" at the end of the statement specifies the level of debugging from 1 to 255. The default is 1. 255 will provide you with a large amount of data.

`debug crypto ipsec 7` will show the IPSec displays debugging information about IPSec connections. As with the debug crypto isakmp 7 command, the number at the end of command is optional and specifies the level of debugging information from 1 to 255.

Wrapping up the Site-to-Site VPN Exercise

Now that you have made additional changes to your configuration, back it up using the procedures learned earlier:

`asa# copy run tftp://[YOUR COMPUTER'S IP ADDRESS]/config _ vpn _ 121.txt`

When you are finished, reload your appliances without saving the changed configuration.

Configuring a Site-to-Site VPN Using the GUI-based Wizard

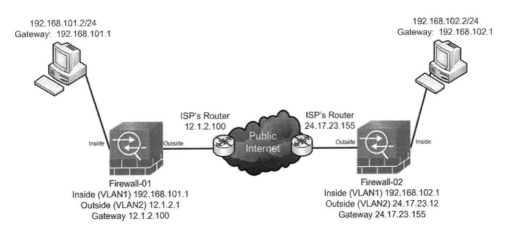

Figure 123: A site-to-site VPN example

The above diagram shows how a site-to-site VPN configuration might look in the real world. Notice the use of public addresses on the outside interfaces (12.1.2.100 and 24.17.23.155). They are used in the diagram purely for demonstration purposes and should not be used in a real-world configuration, unless, of course, your ISP has assigned them to you.

As you go through the following steps, remember that the values on each firewall need to match the partner firewall. For example, the encryption algorithms, timeout values, key lifetimes, and passwords (pre-shared keys) must all match or the VPN will not work. Remember that tunnel-groups refer to the partner's OUTSIDE interface address. Network addresses refer to the entire network address, not just a single interface address. For example, Firewall-01's inside interface address is 192.168.101.1/24, but it is connected to the 192.168.101.0/24 network.

Hands-On Exercise 8.2:
Configuring Site-to-Site VPNs Using the ASDM

In this exercise, as in the previous exercise, you will simulate a VPN connecting two geographically separate offices across the public Internet. Each security appliance can function as both initiator and/or responder. This exercise, however, will be completed using the Adaptive Security Device Manager (ASDM). You will peer one ASA appliance with a second ASA appliance to complete this exercise.

Exercise Requirements

Two Cisco ASA Security Appliances, running software version 9.x. The exercise is written using two 5505s, but should work with any two ASAs. The procedures are similar for earlier software versions as far back as 8.3, but may require slight adjustments. Two computers, each equipped with an Ethernet adapter and configured with a static IP address as indicated in the exercise diagram.

Exercise Diagram

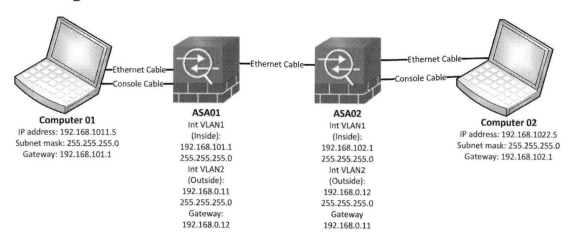

Computer 01
IP address: 192.168.1011.5
Subnet mask: 255.255.255.0
Gateway: 192.168.101.1

ASA01
Int VLAN1
(Inside):
192.168.101.1
255.255.255.0
Int VLAN2
(Outside):
192.168.0.11
255.255.255.0
Gateway:
192.168.0.12

ASA02
Int VLAN1
(Inside):
192.168.102.1
255.255.255.0
Int VLAN2
(Outside):
192.168.0.12
255.255.255.0
Gateway
192.168.0.11

Computer 02
IP address: 192.168.1022.5
Subnet mask: 255.255.255.0
Gateway: 192.168.102.1

Figure 124: Network diagram for the ASDM site-to-site VPN exercise

Exercise Steps

1. In the ASDM menu bar, click on Wizards, then mouse over VPN Wizards and select Site-to-Site VPN Wizard …

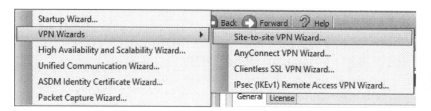

Figure 125:
Starting the Site-to-site
VPN Wizard

2. The Site-to-Site VPN Connection Setup Wizard appears. Click Next.

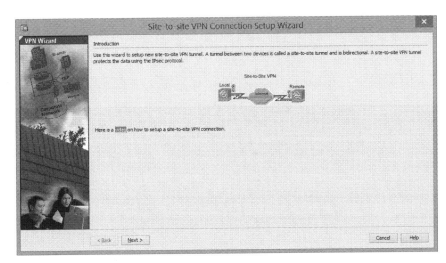

Figure 126:
Introduction to the
Site-to-site VPN Wizard

3. The Peer Device Identification window appears. Enter the outside address of the other ASA. Ensure that the outside interface is selected as the VPN Access Interface. In this screen capture from ASA01, I configured the outside interface address of ASA02. You must reverse the process on ASA02. Click Next.

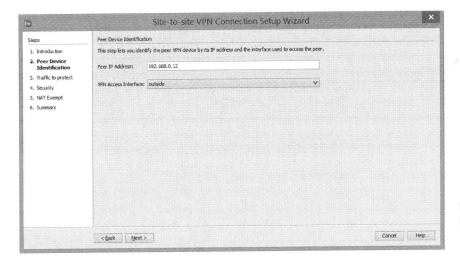

Figure 127:
Peer device identification

4. The *Traffic to protect* window appears. In the first field, enter the network address of the local network. In the second field, enter the network address of the remote network. As you can see in the screen capture, you must also include the subnet mask in CIDR (Classless Inter-Domain Routing) notation (that's the /24 at the end of each network address indicating a 24-bit subnet mask, which in traditional dotted decimal notation would be written 255.255.255.0).

In this screen capture from ASA01, I put the 192.168.101.0/24 network in the local field and the 192.168.102.0/24 network in the remote field. On ASA02, you must reverse the entries. When you're done, click Next.

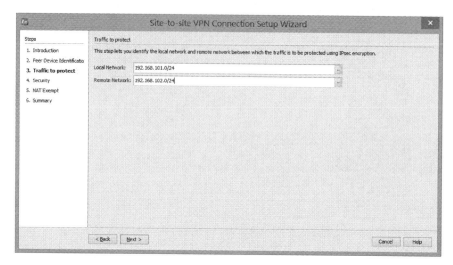

Figure 128:
Traffic to protect

5. The *Security* window appears. For the purpose of this exercise, we'll do the simple configuration. In an enterprise, you probably want to consider using certificates instead of pre-shared keys. Enter *p@ss5678* for the Pre-shared Key. It's important the pre-shared keys match on both ASAs in the VPN. Click Next.

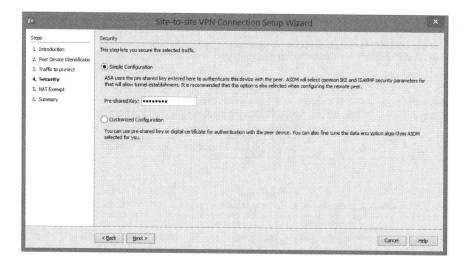

Figure 129:
Configuring VPN security

6. The *NAT Exempt* window appears. For most configurations, you do not want inside traffic to be NATed, so check the box labeled *Exempt ASA side host/network from address translation*. Also, ensure that the inside interface is selected. Click Next.

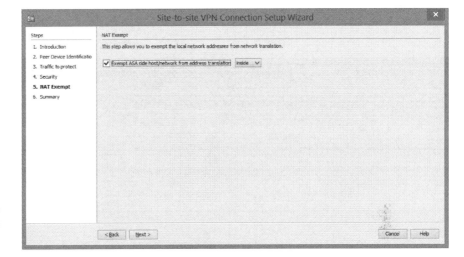

Figure 130:
Configuring the
NAT exemption

7. The *Summary* page appears. Review the settings and, when you're satisfied, click Finish.

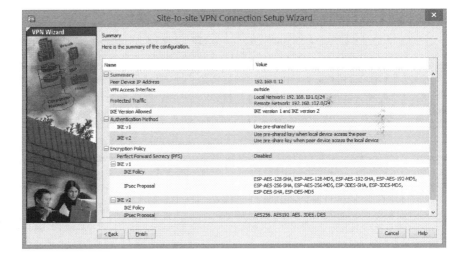

Figure 131:
Site-to-site VPN
setup summary

8. If you've configured your ASA to preview commands before sending them to the device, you'll see another summary of the commands. Click Send, if the preview window appears.

9. In order for the VPN to work, a default route must be in place. If you are using DHCP to obtain IP information on the outside interface, a default route is probably already in place. If not, you must add one. You can check to see if a route is in place by using the CLI command "show route". Look for a line in the output similar to `0.0.0.0 0.0.0.0 (1/0) via 12.1.2.100, outside`.

(Using DHCP to obtain the outside interface addresses in a site-to-site VPN scenario is risky due to the possibility of changing addresses which could result in lost connections for the VPN.)

In this screen capture of the output of "show route", the asterisk (*) by the static route (S) shows the default route.

```
ciscoasa(config)# show route

Codes: L - local, C - connected, S - static, R - RIP, M - mobile, B - BGP
       D - EIGRP, EX - EIGRP external, O - OSPF, IA - OSPF inter area
       N1 - OSPF NSSA external type 1, N2 - OSPF NSSA external type 2
       E1 - OSPF external type 1, E2 - OSPF external type 2
       i - IS-IS, su - IS-IS summary, L1 - IS-IS level-1, L2 - IS-IS level-2
       ia - IS-IS inter area, * - candidate default, U - per-user static route
       o - ODR, P - periodic downloaded static route, + - replicated route

Gateway of last resort is 172.31.0.200 to network 0.0.0.0

S*      0.0.0.0 0.0.0.0 [1/0] via 172.31.0.200, outside
C           172.31.0.0 255.255.255.0 is directly connected, outside
L           172.31.0.1 255.255.255.255 is directly connected, outside
C           192.168.1.0 255.255.255.0 is directly connected, inside
L           192.168.1.1 255.255.255.255 is directly connected, inside
```

Figure 132: Viewing the routing table on the ASA

10. Add a default route, if one does not already exist.

   a. In the ASDM, navigate to Configuration > Device Setup > Routing > Static Routes

   b. On the right-hand side of the window, click the button labeled "Add"

   c. Choose "outside" for the interface

   d. Set the IP address to 0.0.0.0

   e. Configure the Gateway IP to 192.168.0.1
      (If you know you need to use a different gateway address, enter it instead of 192.168.0.1.)

   f. Click OK

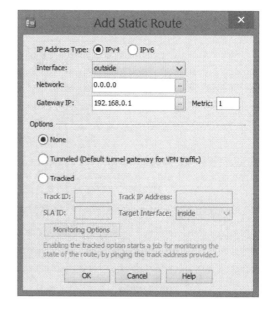

Figure 133:
Adding a default route in the ASDM

11. Confirm the new default route's existence in the routing window (or use the command: **show route** in the command-line interface.

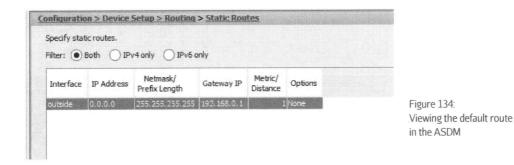

Figure 134:
Viewing the default route
in the ASDM

12. You can verify the existence of the tunnel by choosing Monitoring>VPN.

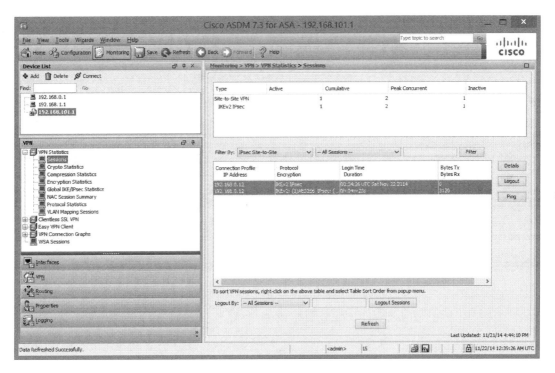

Figure 135: Verifying the existence of the tunnel

13. More information about the connection is available by clicking the Details button on the far right-hand side of the window.

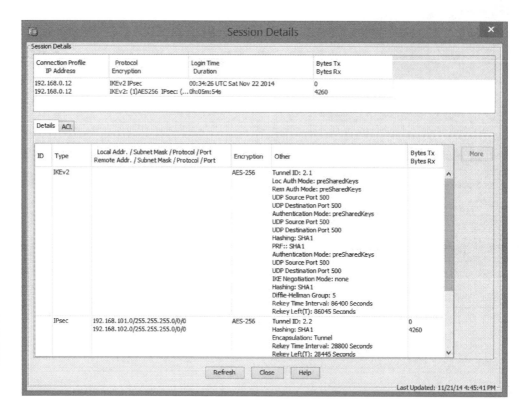

Figure 136: Viewing details about the VPN tunnel

Remote Access VPNs

Remote access VPNs provide a method for mobile users to connect securely to the office network while traveling. The remote access VPN creates a protected tunnel across a non-trusted network such as the public Internet.

Cisco remote access VPNs allow you to connect using several methods:

- Microsoft client using L2TP (Layer 2 Tunneling Protocol)
- Cisco VPN client using IPSec
- Cisco AnyConnect client using SSL
- Clientless SSL VPN which uses a browser and a landing portal

Hands-On Exercise 8.3:
Configuring a Cisco AnyConnect Remote Access VPN

This is a basic VPN configuration for remote workers. In this exercise, you will configure your security appliance to accept inbound remote access connections from clients running the Cisco AnyConnect VPN client software. This exercise will use the ASDM for configuration. When configured to accept inbound remote access connections, the security appliance functions only as a responder.

Exercise Requirements

This exercise requires a Cisco ASA Security Appliance plus a computer acting as the VPN client. I'm using aa ASA 5505 running software version 9.04ED and a computer running Windows 7.

Building this configuration requires the following steps:

- Create a connection profile
- Choose VPN protocols and certificate
- Add a VPN client image
- Configure authentication
- Configure a DHCP pool for remote clients
- Configure name resolution servers
- Enable NAT exemption
- Configure AnyConnect client deployment

In order to complete this exercise, you must also have access to a recent Cisco AnyConnect Secure Mobility VPN client. At the time of this writing, the current version is 3.1.05187. If you have a Cisco support contract, you can download the client from www.cisco.com.

Exercise Diagram

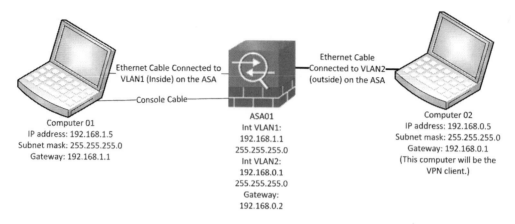

Figure 137: Network diagram for configuring
a remote access VPN

Exercise Prerequisites

Download the AnyConnect client from www.cisco.com. Usually, you should use the most recent image available.

Copy the AnyConnect image into your device's flash memory using TFTP.

Watch the Video

There is a video on my YouTube channel in which I demonstrate the following procedures. Watch the video at http://youtu.be/1oJ1JwYAC8w.

Exercise Steps

1. On computer01, connect to the ASDM (Adaptive Security Device Manager) by entering https://192.168.101.1 in a browser. Authenticate as needed.

2. Click on *Wizards*, then *VPN Wizards*, and then *AnyConnect VPN Wizard*.

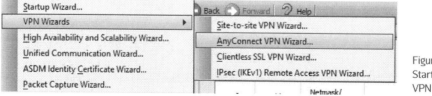

Figure 138:
Starting the AnyConnect
VPN Wizard

3. The AnyConnect VPN Wizard opens. Click *Next*.

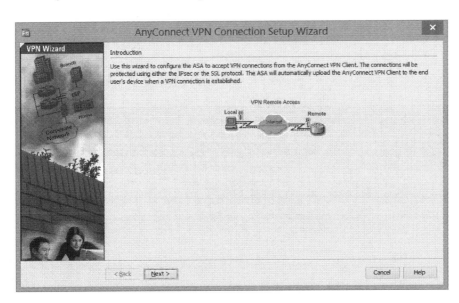

4. The *Connection Profile Identification* page opens. Enter *RemoteUsers* for the Connection Profile Name, accept the default VPN Access Interface of *outside* and click *Next*.

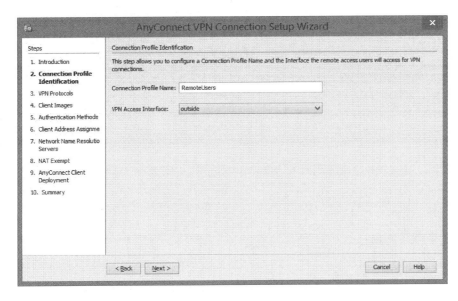

Figure 140:
Connection profile
identification

5. The VPN Protocols page opens, accept the default protocols (SSL and IPSec). A certificate is required, so click the button labeled *Manage*.

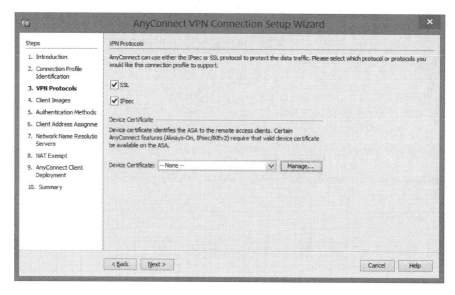

Figure 141: Choosing VPN protocols

6. Under *Manage Identity Certificates*, click *Add*.

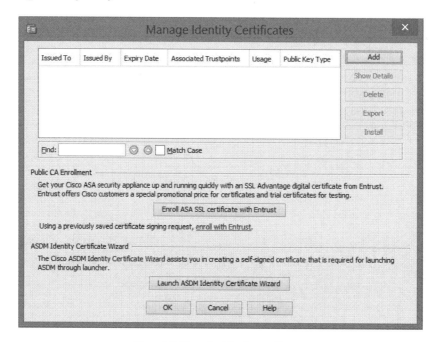

Figure 142: Managing identity certificates

7. Under *Add Identity Certificate,* choose *Add a new identity certificate* and check the box labeled *Generate self-signed certificate.*

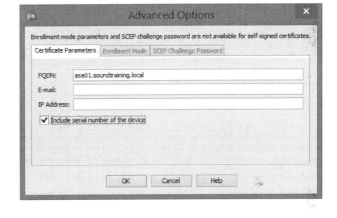

Figure 143:
Adding an identity certificate

8. Click the button labeled *Advanced.*

9. Under *Advanced Options,* confirm or enter your device's fully qualified domain name (FQDN):

   asa01.soundtraining.local

10. Click OK

Figure 144:
Adding certificate parameters

11. Back in the *Add Identity Certificate* window, change the CN to match the fully qualified domain name you just configured.

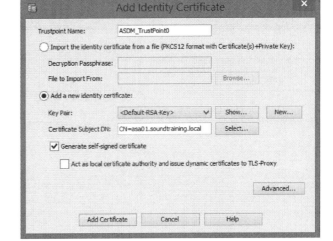

Figure 145:
Changing the common name

12. Click *Add Certificate.* A notification appears letting you know that the certificate enrollment was successful. Click *OK.*

Figure 146:
Successful certificate enrollment

13. Click *OK* in the *Manage Identity Certificates* window.

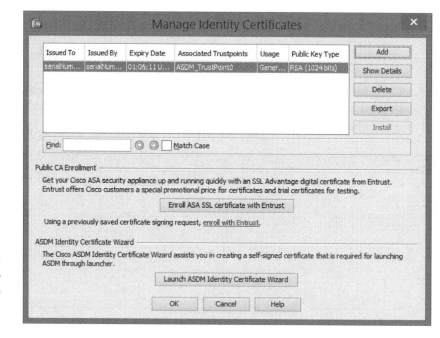

Figure 147:
Viewing the new
identity certificate

14. Notice that the certificate you just created and installed is visible in the Wizard window. Click *Next.*

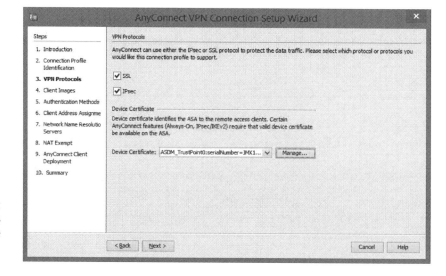

Figure 148:
Viewing the VPN protocols
and the new certificate

15. In the *Client Images* window, add the AnyConnect client image by clicking the button labeled *Add*.

16. Click the button labeled *Browse flash* and select the most recent AnyConnect client image. Click *OK*.

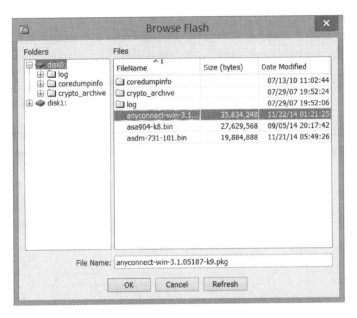

17. In the *Add AnyConnect Client Image* window, click OK.

Figure 150: Adding the client image

18. The image you just added should be visible in the *Client Images* window. Click *Next*.

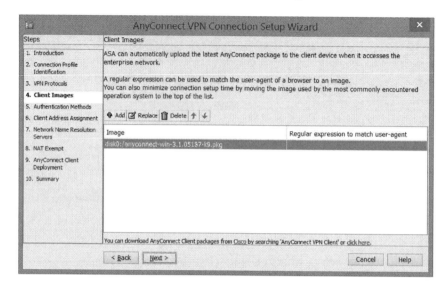

Figure 151: Viewing the newly installed image

19. In the *Authentication Methods* window, add the user *vpnuser* and the password *p@ss1234*. Confirm the password, click *Add* and click *Next*.

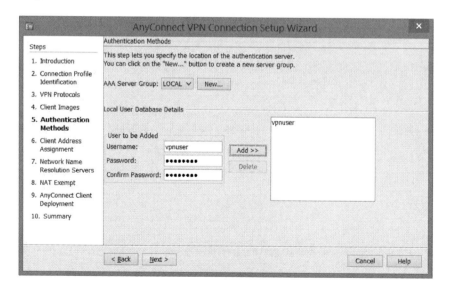

Figure 152: Adding a VPN user

20. In the *Client Address Assignment* window, under the *IPv4 Address Pool* tab, click *New*.

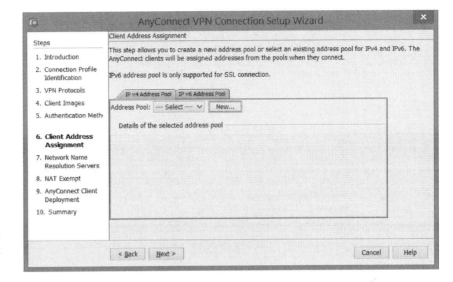

Figure 153:
VPN client address assignment

21. In the *Add IPv4 Pool* window, enter the following parameters:

   a. Name: net-10

   b. Starting IP address: 10.0.0.1

   c. Ending IP address: 10.0.0.10

   d. Subnet Mask: 255.255.255.0

   Click *OK*, then click *Next*.

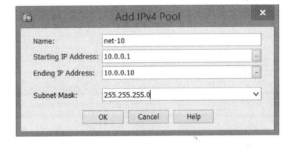

Figure 154: Creating the DHCP pool for VPN clients

22. In the *Network Name Resolutions Servers* window, enter the following parameters:

   a. DNS Servers: 8.8.8.8, 8.8.4.4 (Recall that these are the Google public DNS servers.)

   b. WINS Servers: Leave blank

   c. Domain Name: soundtraining.local

   Click *Next*.

Figure 155: Confirming the DHCP name resolution settings

23. In the *NAT Exempt* window, check the box to *Exempt VPN traffic from Network Address Translation*. Click *Next*.

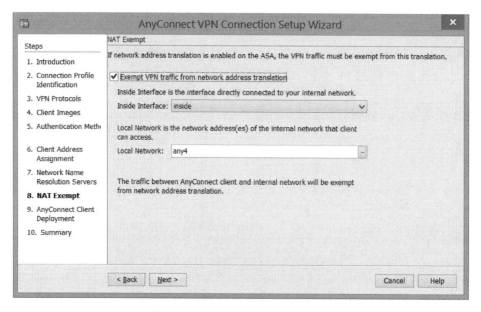

Figure 156: Configuring the NAT exemption

24. Under *AnyConnect Client Deployment,* accept the defaults and click *Next.*

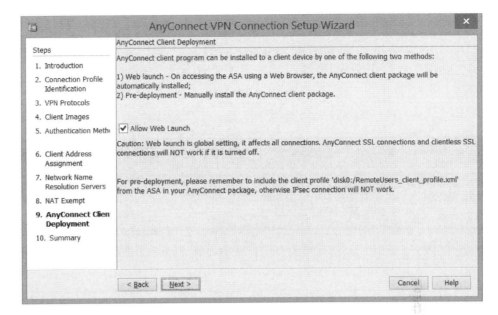

Figure 157:
Configuring AnyConnect
client deployment

25. On the *Summary* page, click *Finish.*

Figure 158:
AnyConnect
VPN configuration
summary page

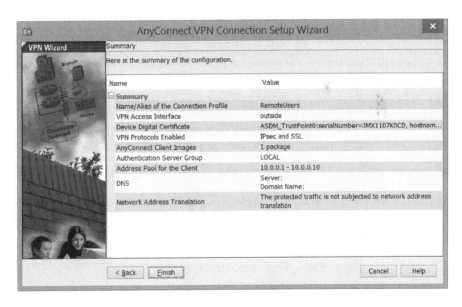

26. If you have enabled command previews, on the *Preview* page, click *Send.*

27. When you're finished, test your configuration by connecting to your VPN from Computer 02.

   a. Open a browser and enter https://192.168.0.1 If you have name resolution enabled, you could also enter the name of your ASA instead of its IP address. Regardless of whether you use an IP address or a name, be sure to use HTTPS or the connection will fail.

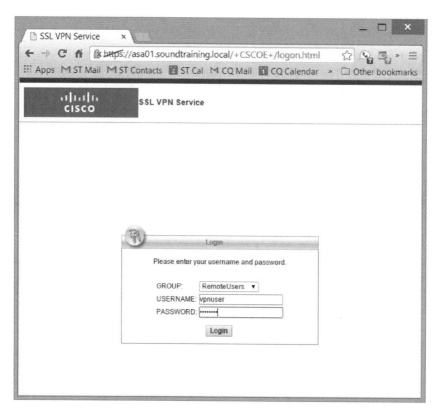

Figure 159: The VPN authentication page

   b. Authenticate using the username *vpnuser* and the password *p@ss1234*

   c. The landing page will attempt to install the AnyConnect VPN client (that's the image you uploaded earlier). The first time you connect, the installation may take a few minutes. I've noticed that it fails with 64-bit browsers, but is successful with 32-bit browsers. If it fails, the landing page provides a link for you to download the desktop installer. It's also possible to configure links to specific resources within your network and include them on the landing page.

Using an AnyConnect Pre-Deploy Package

The Cisco AnyConnect VPN client is also available in a pre-deployment package for use in enterprise software deployment. The Pre-Deploy package is available as an .iso download from Cisco (with a support contract). The .iso includes various Windows AnyConnect clients as .msi installation files. Additionally, the .iso can be burned to removable media and run with a setup file, which is also included.

Hands-On Exercise 8.4:
Configuring ASA VPN Authentication through Active Directory Using RADIUS

In this exercise, you will configure your ASA security appliance to authenticate VPN users against a Microsoft Active Directory domain controller running Windows Server 2012. You can use either the ASDM (Adaptive Security Device Manager) of the command-line to perform this configuration. I find it's easier to do these steps in the command-line, so that's what I'll show you. There is a wizard in the ASDM to help you configure a remote-access VPN, if that's your preference.

Exercise Diagram

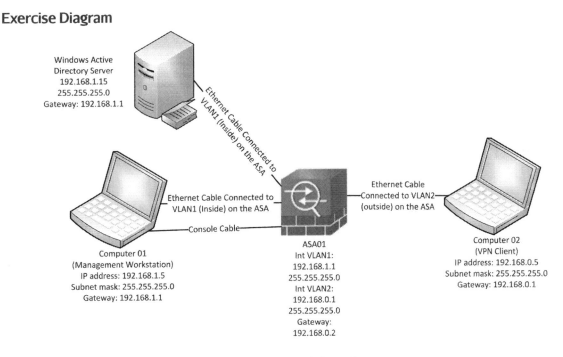

Figure 160: Network diagram for
Active Directory authentication exercises

Exercise Prerequisites

- Administrator-level access to an ASA security appliance with an AnyConnect Remote-Access VPN configured. In this exercise, you will practice adding RADIUS authentication to an existing VPN configuration.

- A local user account on the ASA. If you've been working through the exercises in this book in order, you should have one. Otherwise, use the following command to create one:

  asa01(config)#**username localuser password p@ss1234 privilege 15**

- An Active Directory user account (in the example, the user account is user01).

- A Windows Server computer configured to support RADIUS. (See the previous exercise in chapter five to learn how to install RADIUS support on a computer running Windows Server 2012.)

Watch the Video

There is a video on my YouTube channel in which I demonstrate the following procedures. Watch the video at http://youtu.be/RT5vwTsO98s.

Exercise Steps

The following configuration steps are similar to those shown earlier in chapter five for authenticating admin users through RADIUS.

1. In *global configuration mode*, create an AAA (authentication, authorization, and accounting) server group, specifying RADIUS as the protocol:

   asa01(config)# **aaa-server RADIUSSERVERS protocol radius**

2. Identify the location of the RADIUS server:

   asa01(config-aaa-server-group)# **aaa-server RADIUSSERVERS (inside) host 192.168.1.15**

3. Create the key that will be shared with the RADIUS server. (On the Windows Server 2012 RADIUS server, this is known as the *pre-shared* key.)

   asa01(config-aaa-server-host)# **key p@ss5678**

4. Enter the type of tunnel-group (remote-access) associated with the ASA's VPN users. (In the example, the tunnel-group name is *RemoteUsers*. If you don't know the tunnel-group's name, you can use the command show **run** tunnel to display it.):

   asa01(config-aaa-server-host)#**tunnel-group RemoteUsers type remote-access**

5. Edit the tunnel-group associated with the ASA's VPN users.

   asa01(config-aaa-server-host)# **tunnel-group RemoteUsers general-attributes**

6. Add the authentication-server-group you created in the previous step. (In this example, it's RADIUSSERVERS.)

```
asa01(config-tunnel-general)# authentication-server-group
RADIUSSERVERS LOCAL
```

(Note: Be sure to include the LOCAL statement at the end of the line as a fallback in case the RADIUS server is not reachable. Otherwise, no one will be able to log in.)

7. You can test the configuration from the command-line:

```
asa01# test aaa-server authentication RADIUSSERVERS host 192.168.1.15
username user01 password p@ss1234
```

(In this example, user01 is an existing Active Directory user account.)

Sample RADIUS Authentication Configuration and Test

Figure 161:
Configuring RADIUS
authentication for
VPN users

```
asa01# conf t
asa01(config)# aaa-server RADIUSSERVERS protocol radius
asa01(config-aaa-server-group)# aaa-server RADIUSSERVERS (inside) host 192.168.1.15
asa01(config-aaa-server-host)# key p@ss5678
asa01(config-aaa-server-host)# tunnel-group RemoteUsers type remote-access
asa01(config)# tunnel-group RemoteUsers general-attributes
asa01(config-tunnel-general)# authentication-server-group RADIUSSERVERS LOCAL
asa01(config-tunnel-general)#
asa01# test aaa-server authentication RADIUSSERVERS host 192.168.1.15 username user01 pass
word p@ss1234
INFO: Attempting Authentication test to IP address <192.168.1.15> (timeout: 12 seconds)
INFO: Authentication Successful
asa01#
```

Hands-On Exercise 8.5:
Configuring LDAP Authentication

In this exercise, you will configure your ASA to use Lightweight Directory Access Protocol (LDAP) to authenticate VPN users. Although a detailed explanation of the workings of LDAP is beyond the scope of this book (and well documented elsewhere including RFC 1779 and RFC 2247), here is an explanation of the acronyms used in the following configuration:

- DN: Distinguished Name. The distinguished name is the full path to an object in the directory. Each entity within a directory is identified by its DN, which must be unique within the directory.

- DC: Domain Component. The parts of a DN that are also part of the domain name, in this case *soundtraining* and *local*.

- CN: Common Name. When the object in this attribute is a person, the cn is typically the person's name. Think of CNs as one of the directory objects held within DCs. In this case, *administrator* and *Users*.

Exercise Diagram

The diagram for this exercise is the same as for the previous exercise.

Exercise Prerequisites

The prerequisites are also the same, except that it is not necessary to configure the Windows Server 2012 computer to support RADIUS.

Watch the Video

There is a video on my YouTube channel in which I demonstrate the following procedures. Watch the video at http://youtu.be/p_MoBTqMm_s.

Exercise Steps

1. In global configuration mode, issue the following commands to connect to the LDAP server:

   ```
   aaa-server LDAPSERVERS protocol ldap
   aaa-server LDAPSERVERS (inside) host 192.168.1.15
     ldap-base-dn dc=soundtraining,dc=local
     ldap-scope subtree
     ldap-naming-attribute sAMAccountName
     ldap-login-password p@ss5678
     ldap-login-dn
   cn=administrator,cn=Users,dc=soundtraining,dc=local
     server-type auto-detect
   ```

2. Issue the following commands to enable authentication for VPN users:

   ```
   tunnel-group RemoteUsers general-attributes
   authentication-server-group LDAPSERVERS LOCAL
   ```

3. Test the configuration with the following command:

   ```
   test aaa-server authentication LDAPSERVERS host 192.168.1.15
   username user01 password p@ss1234
   ```

Sample LDAP Authentication Configuration and Test

```
                                    COM5 - PuTTY                            _ □ ×
asa01(config)# aaa-server LDAPSERVERS protocol ldap
asa01(config-aaa-server-group)#
asa01(config-aaa-server-group)# aaa-server LDAPSERVERS (inside) host 192.168.1.15
asa01(config-aaa-server-host)#  ldap-base-dn dc=soundtraining,dc=local
asa01(config-aaa-server-host)#  ldap-scope subtree
asa01(config-aaa-server-host)#  ldap-naming-attribute sAMAccountName
asa01(config-aaa-server-host)#  ldap-login-password p@ss5678
asa01(config-aaa-server-host)#  ldap-login-dn cn=administrator,cn=Users,dc=soundtraining,d
c=local
asa01(config-aaa-server-host)#  server-type auto-detect
asa01(config-aaa-server-host)# tunnel-group RemoteUsers general-attributes
asa01(config-tunnel-general)# authentication-server-group LDAPSERVERS LOCAL
asa01(config-tunnel-general)# test aaa-server authentication LDAPSERVERS host 192.168.1.15
 username user01 password p@$
INFO: Attempting Authentication test to IP address <192.168.1.15> (timeout: 12 seconds)
INFO: Authentication Successful
```

Hands-On Exercise 8.6:
Configuring Kerberos Authentication

In the following exercise, you will configure your ASA to authenticate against an Active Directory server using Kerberos.

Exercise Diagram

The diagram for this exercise is the same as for the previous exercise.

Exercise Prerequisites

The prerequisites for this exercise are the same as for the previous exercise.

Watch the Video

There is a video on my YouTube channel in which I demonstrate the following procedures. Watch the video at http://youtu.be/3YQSbvimKys.

Exercise Steps

1. In global configuration mode, issue the following commands to connect to the AD server:

    ```
    aaa-server ADSERVERS protocol Kerberos

    aaa-server ADSERVERS (inside) host 192.168.1.15

    kerberos-realm SOUNDTRAINING.LOCAL
    ```

    (Obviously, if your Active Directory server is configured with a different Kerberos realm (domain name), you must use it instead of soundtraining.local.)

2. Issue the following commands to enable authentication for VPN users:

   `tunnel-group RemoteUsers general-attributes`

   `authentication-server-group ADSERVERS LOCAL`

3. Test the configuration with the following command:

   `test aaa-server authentication ADSERVERS host 192.168.1.15 username`
   `user01 password p@ss1234`

Kerberos is very sensitive to time. If the ASA's clock is not in sync with the clock on the Windows Server 2012 computer, authentication will fail. If it's necessary to set the clock on the ASA, you can do it manually using the **clock set** command. For example, the following command will set the time to 2:30 p.m. on October 21, 2014:

`clock set 14:30:00 21 oct 2014`

You can also use the clock command to set the timezone and to enable daylight savings time. Use *clock ?* to see available options. On a production system, you'll probably want to use NTP (Network Time Protocol) instead of setting the time manually. If you'd like to know more about NTP, visit http://support.ntp.org. In the following exercise, you will learn how to configure your ASA to synchronize its time with an NTP Stratum 2 server. Stratum 2 servers are preferred over Stratum 1 servers for this type of use due to the increasingly heavy load on Stratum 1 servers and the fact that Stratum 2 servers' accuracy is only slightly degraded from Stratum 1 servers. I've included an exercise showing how to configure Network Time Protocol on the next page.

Sample Kerberos Authentication Configuration and Test

```
asa01(config)# aaa-server ADSERVERS protocol Kerberos
asa01(config-aaa-server-group)# aaa-server ADSERVERS (inside) host 192.168.1.15
asa01(config-aaa-server-host)# kerberos-realm SOUNDTRAINING.LOCAL
asa01(config-aaa-server-host)# tunnel-group RemoteUsers general-attributes
asa01(config-tunnel-general)# authentication-server-group ADSERVERS LOCAL
asa01(config-tunnel-general)# test aaa-server authentication ADSERVERS host 192.168.1.15 u
sername user01 password p@ss$
INFO: Attempting Authentication test to IP address <192.168.1.15> (timeout: 12 seconds)
INFO: Authentication Successful
asa01(config-tunnel-general)#
```

Figure 163: Configuring Kerberos authentication for VPN users

Hands-On Exercise 8.7:
Configuring the ASA as a Network Time Protocol Client

Exercise Diagram

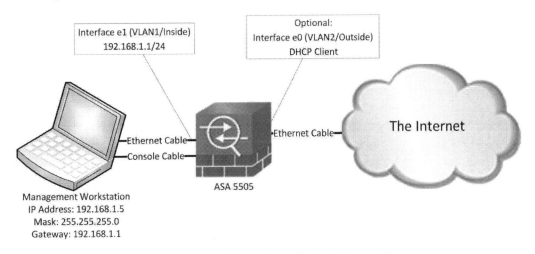

Figure 164: Network diagram for configuring NTP on an ASA

Exercise Prerequisites

This exercise requires that the ASA be Internet-connect. You will need a list of NTP servers, which can be obtained from http://support.ntp.org/bin/view/Servers/WebHome. For the purpose of this exercise, I'll use the NTP servers at 209.59.216.182 and 74.207.242.71. Unfortunately, you must use IP addresses in the ASA's NTP configuration instead of hostnames. Since NTP is maintained by volunteers, you may have to search for a while to find a couple of NTP servers that are up. When I was testing the config for this book, I kept thinking there was something missing from my configuration when, in fact, the problem was that the NTP servers I was trying to use were down. Be persistent.

In a real world setting, I'd be inclined to set up a local Linux or Windows box as an NTP server and point it to pool.ntp.org for time syncing, then point my ASA to the local NTP server. I'm sure Cisco has a reason for requiring an IP address instead of a hostname in the configuration, but it's hard for me to imagine a good reason for doing it that way. Oh well.

Exercise Steps

1. In global configuration mode on your ASA, enter the following commands:

   ciscoasa(config)# **ntp server 209.59.216.182 source outside**

   ciscoasa(config)# **ntp server 74.207.242.71 source outside**

2. Use the *show clock* command to view the date and time.

```
asa01(config)#
asa01(config)# ntp server 209.59.216.182 source outside
asa01(config)# ntp server 74.207.242.71 source outside
asa01(config)# show clock
16:48:45.608 PST Mon Dec 29 2014
asa01(config)#
```

Figure 165: Configuring NTP

You can also use the clock command to set your time zone and daylight savings time preference.

Creating a Web-Based SSL VPN

Remote users are not always able to use their own computers when they need to connect to your LAN. For example, they may be at a client location and need access to the corporate intranet to retrieve email, product documentation, or other information. The Cisco ASA Security appliance supports the use of a clientless SSL VPN connection in which the remote user connects to a highly configurable landing page. The landing page can include a bookmark list of internal URLs, permitted Web applications, and network browsing (if permitted).

Hands-On Exercise 8.8:
Configuring a Web-Based SSL VPN

Exercise Diagram

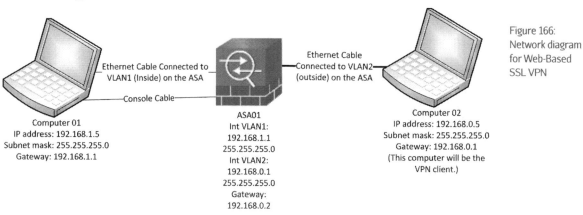

Figure 166: Network diagram for Web-Based SSL VPN

Ethernet Cable Connected to VLAN1 (Inside) on the ASA

Console Cable

Ethernet Cable Connected to VLAN2 (outside) on the ASA

Computer 01
IP address: 192.168.1.5
Subnet mask: 255.255.255.0
Gateway: 192.168.1.1

ASA01
Int VLAN1:
192.168.1.1
255.255.255.0
Int VLAN2:
192.168.0.1
255.255.255.0
Gateway:
192.168.0.2

Computer 02
IP address: 192.168.0.5
Subnet mask: 255.255.255.0
Gateway: 192.168.0.1
(This computer will be the VPN client.)

Exercise Prerequisites

This exercise requires that you configure a user named *user15* with the password *password* on the ASA. Additionally, since this exercise will be conducted using the Adaptive Security Device Manager, you must also ensure that the ASA is configured to support connections from the 192.168.1.0/24 subnet. See chapter four to refresh your memory on configuring support for ASDM.

In this exercise, you will configure a simple Web-based, client-less SSL VPN. The VPN will allow the user to connect to a landing page which will display a single URL for the user.

Exercise Steps

1. Connect to your firewall using ASDM and user15 with the password *password*. In a browser on Computer01, enter https://192.168.1.1 and follow the prompts to get to the ASDM.

2. In the ASDM menu bar, click on Wizards and then mouse over VPN Wizards. In the submenu, click on Clientless SSL VPN Wizard.

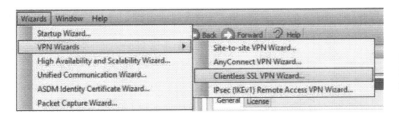

Figure 167:
Starting the clientless
SSL VPN wizard

3. In the SSL VPN Wizard window, click *Next*.

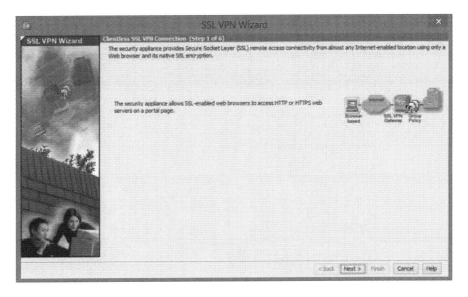

Figure 168: Clientless SSL VPN connection setup

4. On the SSL VPN Interface page, enter a connection profile name of *ssl_vpn_test* and click *Next*.

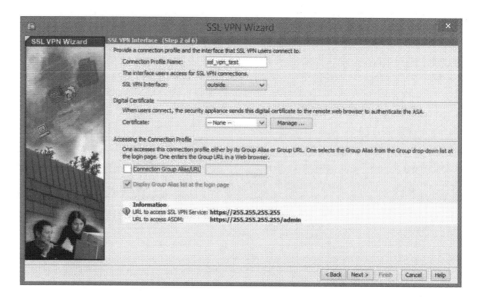

Figure 169:
Configuring interfaces and
connection profiles

5. On the User Authentication page, select the radio button labeled *Authenticate using the local user database* and create a new user named *ssluser* with a password of *p@ss1234*. (Any user you created previously should already be displayed.) Click *Add* to add the new user to the local database.

6. Click *Next*.

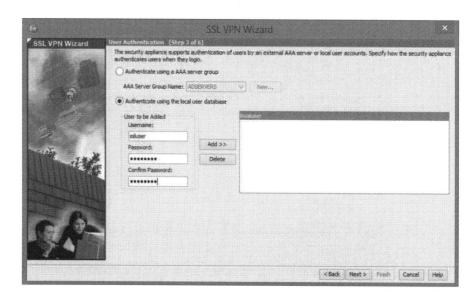

Figure 170:
Adding the SSL VPN user

7. On the Group Policy page, create a new group policy called *test_gp* and click *Next*.

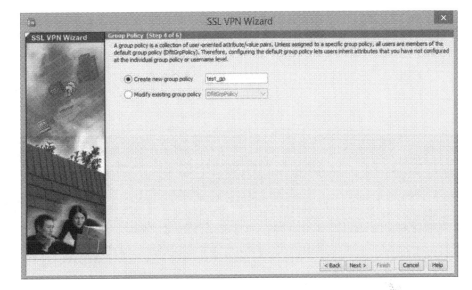

Figure 171:
Setting the SSL VPN group policy

8. On the Bookmark List page, click *Manage* and add a bookmark list to appear on the landing.

   a. On the Configure GUI Customization Objects window, click *Add*

   b. Enter *Test_Bookmark_List* for the bookmark list name and click *Add* to add a bookmark entry.

   c. Click OK to accept the default of *URL with GET or POST method*

   d. Enter *My Website* for the bookmark title and a URL value of http://192.168.1.5.

   e. Click OK as needed to exit the GUI Customization Objects applet

Figure 172:
Adding SSL VPN bookmarks

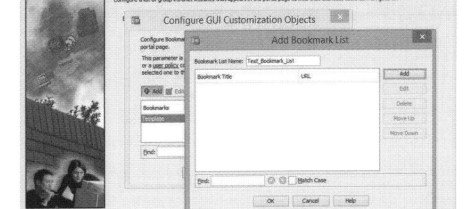

6. Click *Next*.

7. Click *Finish*.

8. Click *Send*.

9. Test the configuration by using Computer02 to connect to the outside interface of the security appliance in a browser (https://192.168.0.1). Remember, it is SSL, so you must use a protocol type of HTTPS.

When you're able to connect successfully, you should see a landing portal page similar to this.

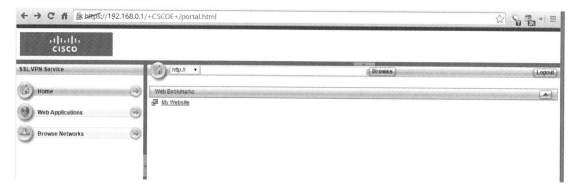

Figure 173: The SSL VPN landing portal

Note the warning in the address bar concerning HTTPS. The reason the browser is complaining about the connection is because I did not install a valid SSL certificate. The connection will work without a certificate, but the browser will throw off a warning. If you want to eliminate the warning, install a certificate.

How to Install an SSL Digital Certificate for Use with an SSL VPN

The use of an SSL digital certificate eliminates the error displayed by browsers when VPN users connect to an SSL-based VPN. SSL digital certificates are available from a variety of vendors.

Summary of Steps

- Generate a new RSA keypair
- Generate the certificate signing request (CSR)
- Upload the CSR to a certificate authority (CA)
- Wait for the CA to send back the certificate
- Install the certificate on the ASA

Hands-On Exercise 8.9:
Installing an SSL Digital Certificate

Exercise Diagram

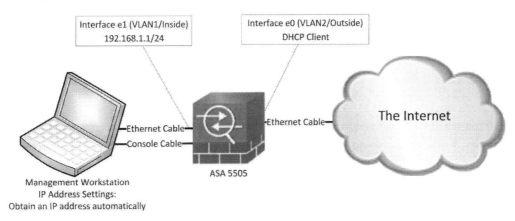

Figure 174: Network diagram for installing an SSL certificate

Exercise Prerequisites

In order to complete this exercise, you will need to submit a certificate signing request (CSR) to a certificate authority (CA). This will require Internet access and usually requires some sort of login account at the CA.

Watch the Video

There is a video on my YouTube channel in which I demonstrate the following procedures. Watch the video at http://youtu.be/kANFvl6yj3w.

Exercise Steps

In this exercise, you will generate and install an SSL digital certificate for use with an SSL-based VPN.

1. In global configuration mode, use the following command to generate a new RSA keypair named mykey.key with a key length (modulus) of 2048 bits:

   ```
   crypto key generate rsa label asa01.soundtraining.net modulus 2048
   ```

2. After generating the keypair, go to the ASDM to complete the remaining steps in this exercise.

3. In the ASDM, go to Configuration>Device Management>Certificate Management> Identity Certificates.

4. Click the button in the upper right-hand corner labeled Add.

5. Select the radio button labeled Add a new identity certificate and choose the key pair that you just created (mykey.key) from the pull-down list.

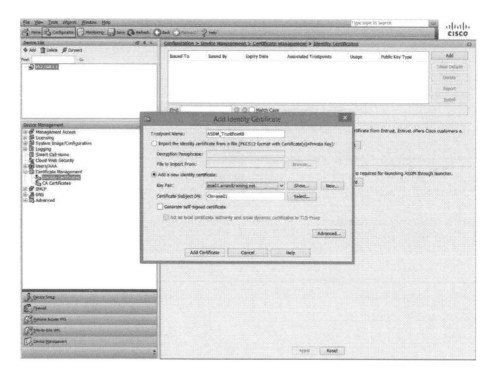

Figure 175:
Adding an identity
certificate

6. You must add various attributes to the certificate. Different Certificate Authorities seem to have different requirements, but what I'm showing you here seems to be fairly universal. Add the attributes by clicking the button labeled *Select* ... and add the Common Name (asa01. soundtraining.net), the Company Name (soundtraining.net), the Country (US), the State (Washington (abbreviations are not permitted), and the Location (Seattle). Of course, feel free to create your own attributes if you wish. When you've finished adding all the attributes, click the button labeled OK.

Figure 176:
Certificate subject DN
(Distinguished Name)

7. Click the button labeled *Add Certificate*. If you have previously configured the ASDM to preview commands before sending them to the device, you'll see a preview window. In the preview window, click the button labeled *Send*.

8. You'll be prompted to save the CSR (Certificate Signing Request) to a file. I usually put the CSR on my desktop just to make it easier to find, but, of course, you can put it anywhere you wish and name it anything you wish.

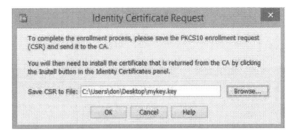

Figure 177: Saving the CSR

9. Next, open the file you just saved with a text editor, such as Notepad, and copy the entire contents of the file.

10. From your management workstation, use a Web browser to go to a certificate authority such as Verisign (www.verisign.com), Comodo (www.instantssl.com), DigiCert (www.digicert.com), or GeoTrust (www.geotrust.com). Follow their steps to submit the CSR, which usually involves creating an account and then copying and pasting the request into a form similar to what you see in the screen capture below.

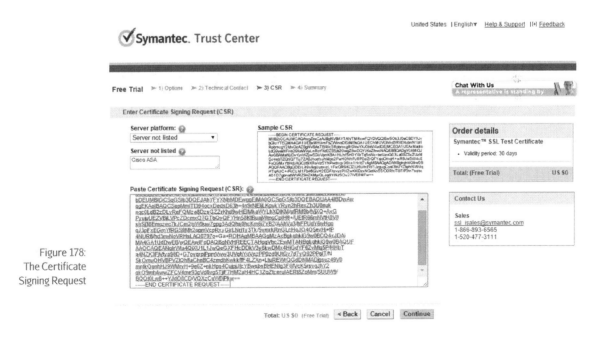

Figure 178: The Certificate Signing Request

Many certificate authorities offer a 30 day free trial, such as the one I used from GeoTrust.

11. After you submit the CSR to the CA, they will email the certificate back to you. The amount of time between when you submit the request and receive the certificate varies from instantly to a day or longer, depending on the CA and the type of certificate you're requesting. The more secure certificates require a longer time to process due to the time required for verification of your identity and the identity of the domain with which you're working. In the case of this free trial certificate, I received the email instantly since there is no verification of identity. (Obviously, you wouldn't want to use such a certificate on a production firewall.) The CA will provide instructions on how to install the certificate, so you should follow those. I'll show you how it's done with this sample cert from GeoTrust.

12. GeoTrust sent the digital identity certificate for asa01.soundtraining.net in an email, plus I had to download an intermediate identity certificate from their website. I saved both on my computer.

13. After you receive the certificate from the CA, reconnect your management workstation to the ASA's inside interface.

14. Reconnect to the ASDM and, once again, go to Configuration>Device Management>Certificate Management, choose CA Certificates, then choose *Add* in the upper right-hand corner.

15. Choose to install from a file. Browse to the location where you saved the downloaded certificate files and select the intermediate certificate file.

Figure 179:
Installing a certificate

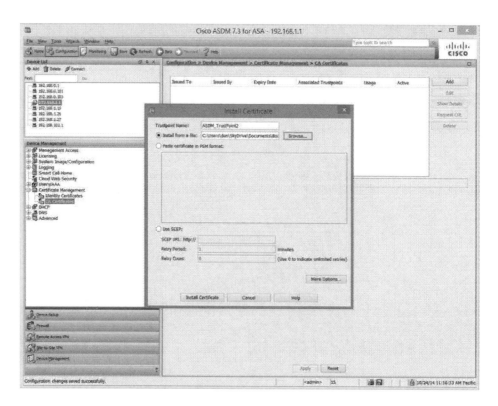

16. Next, choose *Install Certificate*. You'll see a confirmation that the certificate was installed successfully.

17. Now, go back to Identity Certificates under Certificate Management. Select the certificate that you generated earlier (from when you generated the private key).

18. Click on the button labeled *Install* in the upper right-hand corner of the screen.

19. In the *Install Identity certificate* window, browse to the location where you saved the downloaded certificates and choose the identity certificate for the ASA. (In this example, I named it SSLCert.txt.)

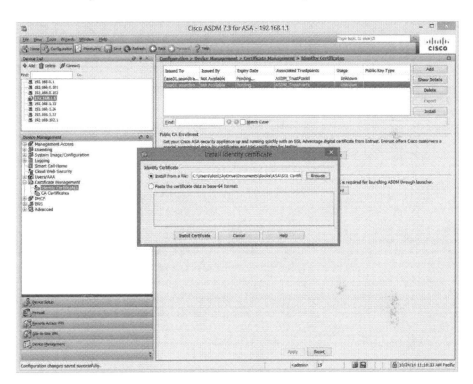

Figure 180:
Installing
the certificate
from a file

20. Click the button labeled *Install Certificate*.

21. You'll receive confirmation that the installation was successful and the information about the certificate should change to reflect the name of the issuer, the expiry date, and the certificate usage.

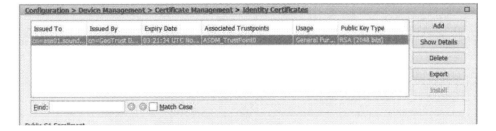

Figure 181:
Adding the identity
certificate

Hands-On Exercise 8.10:
Enabling the SSL Certificate

You must also configure the ASA to actually use the newly installed certificate, otherwise it will continue to use the unverified default certificate and throw off a security error.

Exercise Diagram

The exercise diagram for this exercise is the same as the previous exercise.

Exercise Prerequisites

The prerequisites for this exercise are the same as the previous exercise.

Exercise Steps

1. In the ASDM, go to Configuration>Device Management>Advanced> SSL Settings.

2. On the right-hand side of the window, in the Certificates section, choose the interface where you wish to make connections (probably *outside* since you're configuring a VPN).

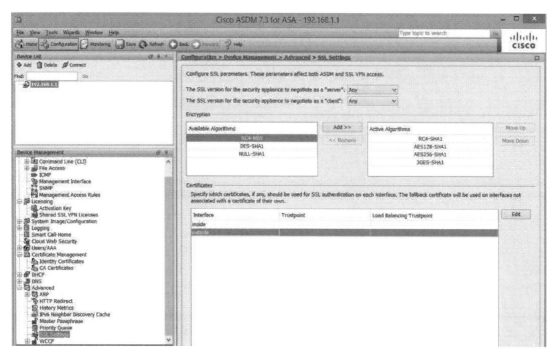

Figure 182: Enabling the certificate

3. Click the button labeled *Edit* and choose your desired Primary Enrolled Certificate, probably the certificate you just installed.

Figure 183:
Selecting the SSL certificate

4. Click OK, then click Apply.

5. You can now test the certificate by connecting to the VPN landing portal in a browser. In order to do that, connect a computer to the ASA's outside interface.

The above steps are required for both ASDM and VPN access using HTTPS. Regardless of the purpose for which you wish to access the security appliance, the SSL certificate must be installed and activated on the desired interface.

Using Internal Names in an SSL Certificate

As you probably noticed, in the screen captures and exercise steps, I used the internal domain soundtraining.local. As of November 1, 2015, the use of internal domain names is no longer supported by the CA/Browser Forum and you'll have to use public domains such as .com, .net, .org, and similar names in order to have a certificate issued to you. For more information about this change, visit https://cabforum.org/internal-names/.

Enhancing the Web VPN Portal with Plug-Ins

Numerous browser plug-ins are available to add functionality to the clientless WebVPN service on the ASA security appliance. Browser plug-ins are separate programs invoked by a Web browser. Such plug-ins perform specific functions such as creating SSH connections or opening a remote desktop connection in a browser window. Many of the plug-ins are tested and redistributed by Cisco. When installed, plug-ins modify the home page of the WebVPN portal, presenting a link for their use.

Plug-in	Plug-in File Name	New Address Field Option	New Main Menu Option
ICA	ica-plugin.zip	ica://	Citrix Client
RDP	rdp-plugin.jar	rdp://	Terminal Servers
SSH, Telnet	ssh-plugin.jar	ssh:// telnet://	SSH Telnet
VNC	vnc-plugin.jar	vnc://	VNC Client

The easiest way to find the plug-ins distributed by Cisco is to log in to the Cisco website with your SmartNet I.D. and search for the particular plug-in you need. For example, in the Cisco website search box type: "rdp-plugin.jar". Many of the plug-ins are licensed under open-source licenses, so if you do not have a SmartNet contract, you may be able to find them by searching various open-source software repositories.

Installing Plug-Ins on the Security Appliance

The plug-ins cannot be installed until WebVPN is configured on the security appliance. Installation of the plug-in requires a running TFTP server. The plug-in should be downloaded to your TFTP server's root directory. After configuring WebVPN on the appliance and downloading the plug-in, perform the following steps:

1. On your security appliance, enter the following command:

   `asa#`**`import webvpn plug-in protocol rdp`**

   `tftp://tftp _ server name or address/rdp-plugin.jar`

2. The appliance will copy the plug-in from the TFTP server to a subdirectory on the device's flash (disk0:/csco_config/97/plugin/)

3. Once the plug-in is installed, links can be created on the user's portal page to various network resources or users with appropriate permissions can simple enter a standard URL to access network resources. For example:

   rdp://192.168.1.2

   ssh://192.168.1.3

   vnc://192.168.1.4

   telnet://192.168.1.5

4. The procedure for installing other plug-ins is similar to that for RDP. When you install the SSH plugin, be careful of the syntax. The SSH plug-in includes both SSH and Telnet. When you enter the plug-in name (ssh,telnet), it must be entered with a comma, but no spaces.

```
import webvpn plug-in protocol ssh,telnet
```

5. A plug-in's existence is not part of the appliance's running-config. In fact, the appliance uses a plug-in based on the plug-in's existence in flash memory (in the disk0:/csco-config/97/plugin directory). To remove a plug-in, use the revert command.

```
revert webvpn plug-in protocol rdp
```

Hands-On Exercise 8.11:
Installing and Removing Plug-Ins

In this exercise, you will install the RDP plug-in to allow remote users to connect to Terminal Servers in your network. You will enable Remote Desktop on your management workstation to verify the configuration.

Exercise Diagram

This exercise uses the same diagram as the previous exercise.

Exercise Prerequisites

This exercise requires a plugin for the Cisco ASA Security Appliance. If you have a Cisco SMARTnet support contract and an encryption entitlement, the plugin can be downloaded for free from the Cisco website. The URL is too long to list here, but do a search on the term "remote access plugins for adaptive security appliance" and you'll find the Cisco download page. If you're reading this on a Kindle, use this link.

Otherwise, you must contact your Cisco reseller.

Exercise Steps

1. Verify that WebVPN is installed on your firewall with the following command in the CLI of your security appliance:

```
ciscoasa#show run webvpn
```

2. On your management workstation, navigate to the Cisco website using the search term indicated above and download the Terminal Service client plugin for ASA. Save it to your TFTP root directory (perhaps c:\myconfigs). Notice that there are several other plugins available, as you can see in the following screen capture.

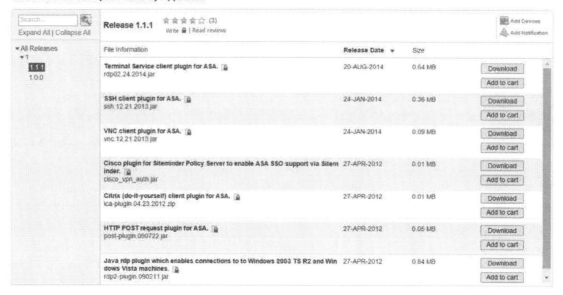

Figure 184: Viewing available plugins for download from Cisco

3. On your security appliance, enter the following commands in the CLI:

   ciscoasa#**import webvpn plug-in protocol rdp**

   tftp://192.168.1.5/rdp-plugin.jar (where 192.168.1.5 is the IP address of your management workstation)

4. View the installed plugin with the following command:

   ciscoasa#**show import webvpn plug-in**

Connecting to an ASA's WebVPN Portal

You will now test configurations by connecting to the security appliance's SSL Web VPN portal.

1. Click on Start, then click on Run and enter the following in the Run dialog box:

   https://192.168.0.1 (where 192.168.0.1 is the outside interface of the security appliance. Also, note the use of HTTPS as the protocol type.)

2. When the WebVPN portal opens in your browser, enter the username *ssluser* with a password of *p@ss1234*.

3. Following authentication, the SSL VPN Service home page will appear. In the address bar at the top of the page, click the down arrow by the protocol type and notice that RDP is now an option, indicating that the plug-in was properly installed.

Important: Remove the webvpn plug-in and URL-list with the following command:

```
ciscoasa#revert webvpn all
```

To Troubleshoot and Test the Configuration

If your Web and SSL VPN connections fail, the following commands may be helpful in troubleshooting:

- **management-access inside** allows you to ping the inside interface of the security appliance.
- **show vpn-sessiondb detail web** displays connection information for Web-based VPN clients.
- **show vpn-sessiondb detail svc** displays connection information for SSL VPN clients.

CHAPTER 9:
De-Militarized Zones (DMZs)

"The problem with troubleshooting is that trouble shoots back."

—Unknown

Understanding a De-Militarized Zone

A De-Militarized Zone or DMZ allows you to isolate certain groups of hosts from other groups of hosts. One example of the use of a DMZ would include creating a separate zone for Internet-accessible servers such as a Web server. Another use of a DMZ would be in a home office environment where home computers need to be isolated from business computers.

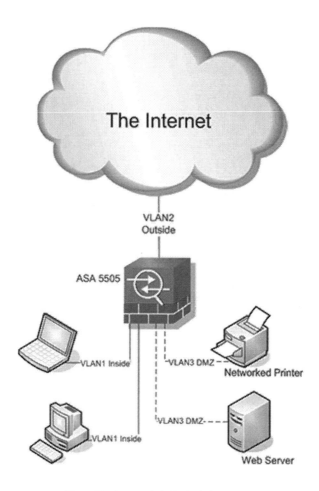

Figure 185: A network design including a DMZ

Notice in the example that the Web server and the networked printer are both located in the DMZ. Such a configuration would allow printing from both the Web server in VLAN3 as well as from any host in VLAN1. In a typical configuration, access to VLAN1 would be highly restricted which would prevent hosts such as the VLAN3 Web server from using the networked printer, if it were located in VLAN1.

In addition to workplace DMZs, a DMZ could also be used in a home office environment to isolate personal systems such as game consoles and family computers from home office computers, thus limiting the exposure of the home office computers to malware including, but not limited to worms and viruses.

Hands-On Exercise 9.1:
Configuring a DMZ

In this exercise, you will configure a DMZ VLAN in which the HTTP server in the DMZ VLAN is accessible to hosts on the business VLAN, but not the other way around.

Exercise Diagram

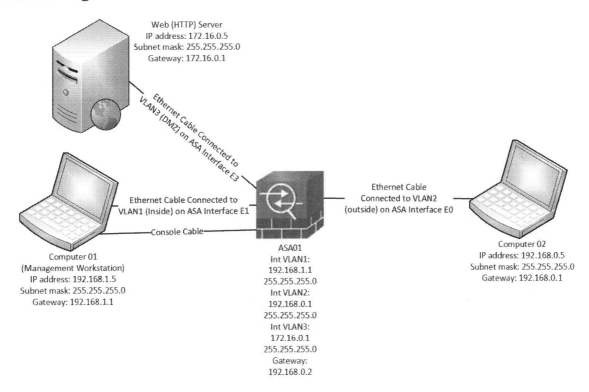

Web (HTTP) Server
IP address: 172.16.0.5
Subnet mask: 255.255.255.0
Gateway: 172.16.0.1

Ethernet Cable Connected to VLAN3 (DMZ) on ASA Interface E3

Ethernet Cable Connected to VLAN1 (Inside) on ASA Interface E1

Console Cable

Ethernet Cable Connected to VLAN2 (outside) on ASA Interface E0

Computer 01
(Management Workstation)
IP address: 192.168.1.5
Subnet mask: 255.255.255.0
Gateway: 192.168.1.1

ASA01
Int VLAN1:
192.168.1.1
255.255.255.0
Int VLAN2:
192.168.0.1
255.255.255.0
Int VLAN3:
172.16.0.1
255.255.255.0
Gateway:
192.168.0.2

Computer 02
IP address: 192.168.0.5
Subnet mask: 255.255.255.0
Gateway: 192.168.0.1

Figure 186: Network diagram to configure a DMZ

Exercise Prerequisites

This exercise requires three computers: a management workstation connected to the ASA's inside interface, a Web server connected to the DMZ interface, and a computer with a Web browser connected to the ASA's outside interface.

You will also need to download the Abyss Web server software from http://www.aprelium.com/abyssws/download.php or, if you prefer, you can use a different HTTP server.

Computer02 must be configured so its firewall allows it to respond to pings.

The ASA must be configured to allow ICMP packets to pass. If necessary, enter the following commands, in global configuration mode, to permit ping packets to pass through the firewall:

```
access-list 101 permit icmp any any echo-reply

access-group 101 in interface outside
```

Watch the Video

There is a video on my YouTube channel in which I demonstrate the following procedures. Watch the video at http://youtu.be/eeTZZN5U858.

Exercise Steps

1. Reload your ASA with the privileged mode command "`reload`" to return it to a pristine configuration. (Remember what we did right before all of the VPN exercises?) Do NOT save the existing configuration.

2. On your management workstation, click on Start, then click Run. Enter `https192.168.1.1` in the Run dialog window to connect to your ASA. Follow the prompts, using the password *p@ss5678* when required to connect to the ASDM console.

3. Click through the security warnings in order to establish a connection with the ASDM (Adaptive Security Device Manager).

4. Navigate to Configuration>Device Setup>Interfaces. Notice in the Interfaces window that there are two interfaces already configured: An inside interface and an outside interface. If your device has more than two interfaces configured, delete any interface NOT named "inside" or "outside".

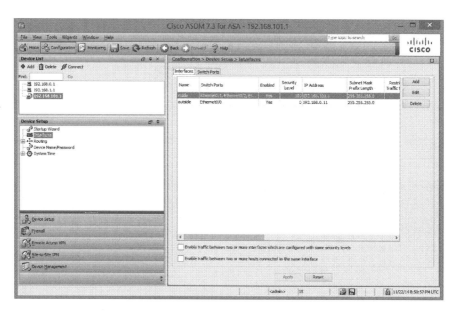

Figure 187:
Configuring a DMZ
in the ASDM

5. You will now build a DMZ from scratch. On the right-hand side of the console, click on the button labeled Add.

6. The Add Interface window appears. In the Switch Ports section, under Available Switch Ports, select Ethernet0/3 and click the button labeled Add to add Switch Port Ethernet 0/3 to the Selected Switch Ports list on the right. Click OK if you receive a Change Switch Port warning. Do the same thing for Switch Port Ethernet 0/4.

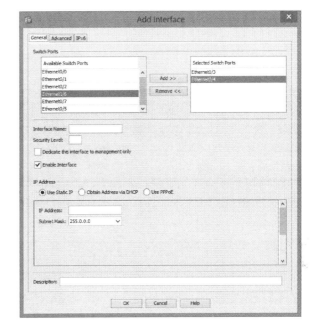

Figure 188:
Assigning ports to the DMZ

7. Ensure that the check box labeled Enable Interface is checked.

8. If your ASA 5505 is licensed with the Base License, it supports only two fully functional interfaces. By configuring a third interface (the DMZ VLAN), you will exceed the licensed number of interfaces unless you limit access from one of the three interfaces to one of the other interfaces. In this exercise, you will prevent hosts on the DMZ VLAN from accessing resources on the Inside VLAN.

9. At the top of the Add Interface window, click on the Advanced tab.

10. In the middle of the window, in the Block Traffic section, use the pull-down menu to block traffic from this interface to vlan1 (inside).

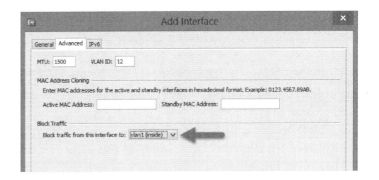

Figure 189: Restricting traffic to VLAN 1

11. Return to the General page by clicking the tab at the top of the page.

Figure 190:
Reviewing the DMZ
port assignments

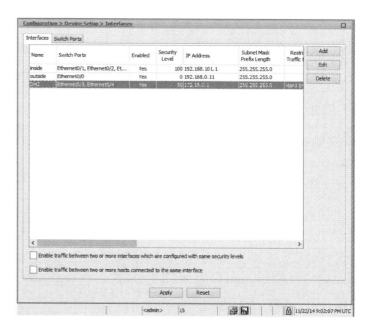

12. Enter DMZ for the Interface Name.

13. Enter 50 for the Security Level.

14. In the IP Address section, ensure that the radio button labeled Use Static IP is selected.

15. Enter 172.16.0.1 for the IP address and select 255.255.255.0 for the subnet mask.

16. Optionally, enter a description at the bottom of the page.

17. At the bottom of the page, click the button labeled OK

18. At the bottom of the window, click the button labeled Apply. Review the commands in the Preview CLI Commands window, then click Send.

19. Exit from the ASDM.

Figure 191: Applying the port assignments

20. Test your DMZ VLAN by connecting your management workstation's Ethernet cable to SwitchPort 0/3 (e3) on your ASA.

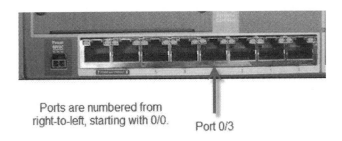

Ports are numbered from right-to-left, starting with 0/0.

Port 0/3

Figure 192:
The interfaces on the back of the ASA 5505

21. On the Web server, click on Start>Run and enter cmd in the Run dialog window to open a command window. Enter the command *ping 192.168.0.5* to test a connection with computer02. The ping will fail, because the ASA is not properly configured with Port Address Translation for the DMZ VLAN. (Also, check to be sure the Web server is configured according to the exercise diagram above.)

```
C:\WINDOWS\system32\cmd.exe

C:\Users\don>ping 192.168.0.5

Pinging 192.168.0.5 with 32 bytes of data:
Request timed out.
Request timed out.
Request timed out.
Request timed out.

Ping statistics for 192.168.0.5:
    Packets: Sent = 4, Received = 0, Lost = 4 (100% loss),

C:\Users\don>_
```

Figure 193:
Testing the VLAN configuration

22. Configure PAT for the DMZ. (In this configuration, *subnet 0 0* represents any IP address and mask. You might want to make a more restrictive statement by explicitly specifying the DMZ subnet.) On the ASA, execute the following commands:

```
ciscoasa(config)# object network DMZ _ outside
ciscoasa(config-network-object)# subnet 0 0
ciscoasa(config-network-object)# nat (DMZ,outside) dynamic interface
```

In a real-world setting, a DMZ could contain resources such as a printer or a Web server that hosts on the Inside VLAN would need to access. In this section of the exercise, you will configure the computer connected to the DMZ VLAN as a Web server. You will then configure the firewall to allow access to the DMZ VLAN from both the Inside VLAN and the outside VLAN. Hosts on the Inside VLAN will be protected from hosts on the DMZ VLAN because traffic will not be permitted to flow from the DMZ VLAN to the Inside VLAN.

Hands-On Exercise 9.2:
Installing the Abyss Web Server Software

You will now install a Web server application on your HTTP server connected to the DMZ VLAN using the following commands. (The Abyss Web server was chosen for this exercise because it is small and quick to install. I have not tested it in a production environment and do not recommend it without testing and evaluation. You can certainly use other Web server software such as Apache (www.apache.org) or Internet Information Server (IIS), which is included with Windows.)

1. On your management workstation, click on Start, then click on Run.

2. In the Run dialog box, enter http://www.aprelium.com/abyssws/download.php

3. On the download page, find and download the correct software for your platform, probably the version for Microsoft Windows

4. Install and configure, using defaults, the Abyss web server software.

5. Following installation, ensure that the web server software is running on your computer.

6. Some PCs may be configured with the Windows firewall (or another firewall such as Zone Alarm). If so, a Windows Security Alert may appear. Click Allow Access. (You may also have to specify the network (Public or Private).)

Figure 194: Allowing access for the Abyss Web Server

7. Confirm that your webserver is working by clicking Start, then Run. In the Run dialog window, enter http://localhost. You should see the Abyss default page.

Welcome to Abyss Web Server

Abyss Web Server is running correctly on your system. You should now change this page with yours.

Please include in your web pages (at least the first) the *'Powered by Abyss Web Server'* banner to promote the use of the software.

Abyss Web Server - Copyright © 2001-2014 Aprelium - All rights reserved

Figure 195: The Web server's default home page

Hands-On Exercise 9.3:
Allowing Inside Hosts and Internet Hosts Access to the DMZ Web Server

In the following exercise, you will configure network objects and access-control lists, and static NAT to allow Internet hosts to initiate connections with hosts in the DMZ.

Exercise Diagram
This exercise uses the same diagram as the previous exercise.

Exercise Prerequisites
There are no additional prerequisites for this exercise.

Exercise Steps

1. Create the network object *web-server-fromOutside* for the Web server at 172.16.0.2 and create a static NAT statement to forward www traffic on the outside interface to the host in the DMZ

   ```
   ciscoasa(config)# object network web-server-fromOutside
   ciscoasa(config-network-object)# host 172.16.0.5
   ciscoasa(config-network-object)# nat (DMZ,outside) static interface
   service tcp www www
   ```

2. Create the network object *web-server-fromInside* for the Web server at 172.16.0.2 and create a static NAT statement to forward www traffic on the inside interface to the host in the DMZ

   ```
   ciscoasa(config)# object network web-server-fromInside
   ciscoasa(config-network-object)# host 172.16.0.5
   ciscoasa(config-network-object)# nat (DMZ,inside) static interface
   service tcp www www
   ciscoasa(config)#
   ```

3. Create the ACL *OutsidetoDMZ* to allow www traffic to flow against the security level from any source to the host at 172.16.0.2 and apply it to inbound traffic on the outside interface.

   ```
   ciscoasa(config)# access-list OutsidetoDMZ extended permit tcp any
   host 172.16.0.5 eq www
   ciscoasa(config)# access-group OutsidetoDMZ in interface outside
   ```

Here's what the configuration should look like in the command line:

```
asa01(config)# object network web-server-fromOutside
asa01(config-network-object)# host 172.16.0.5
asa01(config-network-object)# nat (DMZ,outside) static interface service tcp www www
asa01(config-network-object)# object network web-server-fromInside
asa01(config-network-object)# host 172.16.0.5
asa01(config-network-object)# nat (DMZ,inside) static interface service tcp www www
asa01(config-network-object)# access-list OutsidetoDMZ extended permit tcp any host 172.16.0.5 eq www
asa01(config)# access-group OutsidetoDMZ in interface outside
asa01(config)#
```

Figure 196: The DMZ VLAN's configuration example

4. Test the configuration by attempting to connect to the Web server from both the outside network using your ASA's outside address and from the inside network using your ASA's inside address.

5. Now that you have made additional changes to your configuration, save it to flash memory and back it up using the procedures learned earlier:

```
ciscoasa# wr
```

```
ciscoasa# copy run tftp://[YOUR PC's IP ADDRESS]/config _ dmz.txt
```

Hands-On Exercise 9.4:
Using the ASDM to Configure a DHCP Server

In the real world, you might want DHCP enabled on your DMZ VLAN to simplify the process of connecting a laptop to the DMZ for testing or maintenance. In the following exercise, you will configure a DHCP server for the DMZ VLAN using the Adaptive Security Device Manager.

Exercise Diagram
This exercise uses the same diagram as the previous exercise.

Exercise Prerequisites
There are no additional prerequisites for this exercise.

Exercise Steps
1. In the ASDM console, in the menu bar at the top of the console, click on Configuration, then in the lower left-hand corner of the console window click on Device Management. In the properties list, expand DHCP and select DHCP Server.

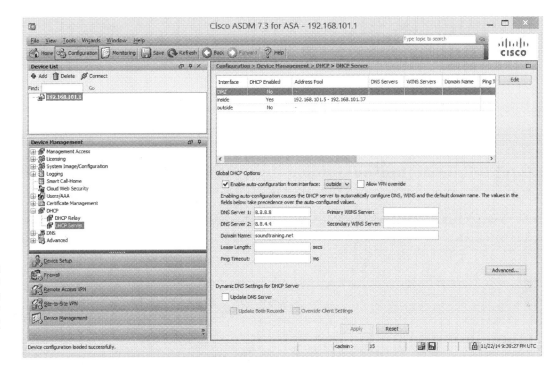

Figure
197:
Setting up
DHCP for
the DMZ

2. Notice in the DHCP Server window, in the DHCP Server section, the three interfaces are listed, but only one has an address pool configured.

3. Select the DMZ interface and click the Edit button immediately to the right of the DHCP Server section. The Edit DHCP Server window will appear.

   a. Check the box labeled Enable DHCP Server.

   b. For the DHCP Address Pool settings, enter 172.16.0.11 to 172.16.0.20.

   c. Toward the bottom of the Optional Parameters section, check the box labeled Enable auto-configuration on interface: and select *Outside* from the pull-down menu.

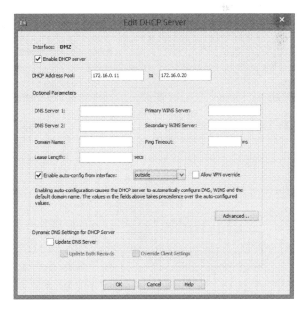

Figure 198: Configuring the DMZ's DHCP pool

4. Click the button labeled Advanced ...

5. On the Advanced DHCP Options page, select Option Code 3(Router).

6. In the Option Data section, in the field labeled Router 1, enter 172.16.0.1. Leave the field labeled Router2 blank.

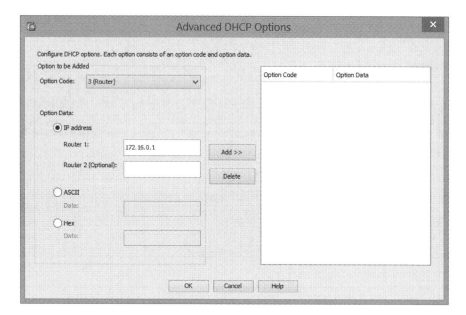

Figure 199:
Adding the router option
to the DHCP server

7. Click Add, then click OK.

8. Click OK at the bottom of the Edit DHCP Server window.

9. Click Apply at the bottom of the Configuration Properties window and click Send to send the changes to the security appliance.

10. Test your DHCP Server configuration. Connect computer01 to SwitchPort 0/4 on your security appliance, click Start, then click Run. In the Run dialog window, type cmd to open a command window.

11. In the command window, type ipconfig to display your current IP address. It will most likely be something other than an address on the 172.16.0.0/24 subnet. It might be on the 192.168.101.0/24 or the 169.254.0.0/16 subnet.

12. Ensure computer01 is configured to obtain an IP address automatically.

13. Now, type ipconfig /renew to request a new IP address. After a few seconds, you should see an IP address of 172.16.0.2 and a default gateway of 172.16.0.1.

CHAPTER 10:
Filtering Content

"I believe that professional wrestling is clean and everything else in the world is fixed."

—Frank Deford

Options for Filtering Content and Threat Detection

There are many types of traffic or content that you may wish to filter as part of your security strategy. For example, you may wish to filter certain types of TCP/IP requests to minimize the effect of certain types of attacks. You might also want to limit the types of dynamic content permitted into your network.

Additionally, the ASA Security Appliance, even with the base license, provides a very basic IPS (Intrusion Prevention System) and IDS (Intrusion Detection System).

Preventing IP Spoofing

IP Spoofing occurs when a packet uses an incorrect source address to conceal its actual source. Unicast Reverse Path Forwarding (Unicast RPF) looks at the source IP address and compares it to the routing table to ensure its source address corresponds to the correct source interface before forwarding the packet.

For example, if a packet enters the outside interface with an IP address associated with the inside interface, the security appliance will drop the packet.

To configure Unicast RPF, use the following command in global configuration mode:

ip verify reverse-path interface [name of interface]

```
asa01(config)# ip verify reverse-path interface ?

configure mode commands/options:
Current available interface(s):
  inside    Name of interface Vlan1
  outside   Name of interface Vlan2
asa01(config)# ip verify reverse-path interface outside
asa01(config)#
```

Figure 200:
IP verify reverse
path lookup

Preventing Fragmented Packets

The security appliance allows up to 24 fragments per IP packet by default. Additionally, it allows up to 200 packets awaiting reassembly. DoS (Denial of Service) attacks often use fragmented packets. Unless you have an application that uses fragmented packets (such as NFS (Network File System) over UDP), do not allow packet fragments through the firewall.

To block fragmented packets, use the following global configuration mode command:

fragment chain 1

```
configure mode commands/options:
  <1-8200>  Maximum number of elements in a fragment set, default is 24
asa01(config)# fragment chain 1
asa01(config)#
```

Figure 201: Limiting fragmented packets

Shunning (Blocking) Unwanted Connections

If you spot a host executing an attack against your network, perhaps by noticing undesirable activity in system logs, you can block their IP address manually by using the shun command. Use the following command in global configuration mode: **shun [source IP address]**

```
asa01(config)# shun ?

exec mode commands/options:
  Hostname or A.B.C.D  Specify source IP address of a mischievous host
asa01(config)# shun 172.31.255.200
Shun 172.31.255.200 added in context: single_vf
Shun 172.31.255.200 successful
asa01(config)#
asa01(config)# no shun 172.31.255.200
asa01(config)#
```

Figure 202: Using the shun command

Notice in the screen capture that I used the *no shun* command to turn the shun off.

Using the shun command with only the source IP address blocks all future connections from the shunned host, but does not drop the current connection. If you want to do that, you must also specify the destination address, source and destination port numbers, and the protocol.

In the following screen capture, I chose to shun tcp packets on port 80 from the source host at 172.31.255.200 going to the destination host at 192.168.255.4 on port 8080.

```
asa01(config)# shun 172.31.255.200 192.168.255.4 80 8080 tcp
Shun 172.31.255.200 added in context: single_vf
Shun 172.31.255.200 successful
asa01(config)#
```

Figure 203:
Using shun with options

Intrusion Prevention

IPS (Intrusion Prevention Service) detects and processes two types of intrusions:

- Information: Gathering information to prepare for an attack
- Attack: Actually attempting to enter your network

The ASA includes pre-configured signatures that define the type of intrusion. An ASA with the AIP SSM (Advanced Inspection and Prevention Security Service Module or Card) offers much more extensive threat detection and prevention. For more information, perform this search "site:cisco.com aip ssm".

To configure IP auditing, use the global configuration command *ip audit*. You must specify an audit policy name, the type of auditing (info or attack), and the action to be taken when matching signatures are detected. Possible actions include alarm, drop, and reset.

- Alarm generates a system message
- Drop drops the packet
- Reset not only drops the packet, it also closes the connection.

In addition to configuring the audit policy, you must also apply the auditing to an interface. In the following screen capture, I created an audit policy named *INFOTEST* to monitor for informational signatures and another audit policy named *ATTACKTEST* to monitor for attack signatures. Both policies were configured to send a system message, drop the packet, and reset the connection.

I applied both policies to the ASA's outside interface.

```
asa01(config)# ip audit name INFOTEST info action alarm reset
asa01(config)# ip audit name ATTACKTEST attack action alarm reset
asa01(config)# ip audit interface outside INFOTEST
asa01(config)# ip audit interface outside ATTACKTEST
asa01(config)#
```

Figure 204: IP auditing configuration

URL Filtering

The Cisco security appliance family supports URL filtering in conjunction with a separate server running WebSense. Websense Enterprise is supported on the Cisco ASA Security Appliance. It can filter HTTP, HTTPS, and FTP.

```
asa01(config)# url-server (inside) host 192.168.0.41 protocol tcp
asa01(config)# filter url http 0 0 0 0
asa01(config)#
```

Figure 205: URL filtering configuration

In the example, URL filtering is enabled for all traffic (0 0 0 0). A Websense host (the default) located at 192.168.0.41 on the inside DMZ will handle the filtering. Requests are sent to the Websense host using TCP.

For more information about Websense, visit www.websense.com.

Cloud Web Security

Cisco also offers a product called Cloud Web Security (CWS), a Software as a Service (SaaS) product which provides security and control for the enterprise. CWS can integrate with an ASA Security Appliance and provide a variety of protections including zero-day defense, analysis of security intelligence, application control, and other services. For more information about CWS, visit http://www.cisco.com/c/en/us/products/security/cloud-web-security.

Dynamic Content Filtering

Although Web-based scripting such as Javascript and ActiveX can create a rich experience for the end user, such forms of active or dynamic content can also be used to compromise systems. The security appliance can be configured to block such content by commenting out such code in the HTML source.

Hands-On Exercise 10.1:
Filtering Dynamic Content

In this exercise, you will connect to a website constructed with Java applets. You will then implement Java filtering on your security appliance to prevent such applets from running.

Exercise Diagram

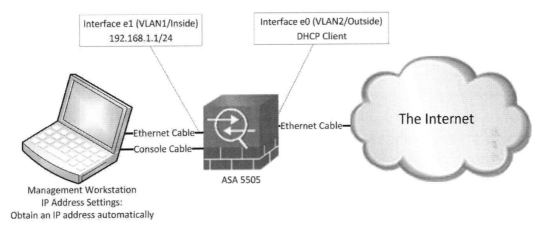

Figure 206: Network diagram for content filtering exercise

Exercise Prerequisites

You must have the ASA configured to support Internet connections as described in chapter one. You must also have a workstation connected to the inside interface on the ASA.

Exercise Steps

1. With your test computer connected to an inside interface on the ASA and the outside interface connected to the public Internet, connect to the http://www.realapplets.com/applets/ realinvaders/default.asp (You may need to tell your browser to run Java applets. I strongly recommend doing this on a test computer and not on your production system.)

2. Go ahead and play a game of Real Invaders. Run it for long enough to see it work.

3. Filter all Java applets in HTTP traffic from any source to any destination with the following command:

```
ciscoasa(config)# filter java 80 0 0 0 0
```

Figure 207:
Filtering java

```
asa01(config)# filter java 80 0 0 0 0
asa01(config)# _
```

In this configuration, 80 represents HTTP traffic, the first two zeros represent any source (the host who initiated the connection) IP address and mask and the second two zeros represent any destination (the website) IP address and mask.

4. Clear your browser's cache. (In Internet Explorer, you can do this by going to Tools>>Internet Options and deleting your browsing history. In Firefox, you can do this by going to Tools>>Options>>Privacy and clicking the link to clear your recent history.)

5. Refresh the applet page. The Java applet should no longer function.

6. Right-click in a blank area of the page and choose View Source or View Page Source. Note that the Java applet has been commented out by the firewall.

You can perform similar procedures to filter ActiveX content.

Auditing for Vulnerabilities Using Port Scanning

Port scanning is a process in which utilities such as nmap, Super Scan, Angry IP, and others are used to test an IP host to discover information about the host including which ports are open and available for connection and the type of operating system in use on the host. Firewalls, when properly configured, help prevent the disclosure of such information during a port scan.

Nmap, for "Network Mapper", is generally regarded as the most popular port scanner. Originally written for UNIX, it is now also available for the Windows platform. Nmap is extremely well-documented at http://insecure.org/nmap. As with any software used in security scanning, care must be taken to ensure that your scans are seen as security audits and not a reconnaissance attack.

Hands-On Exercise 10.2:
Analyzing Potential Vulnerabilities with Port Scanning

In this exercise, you will use the port scanner Nmap (Network Mapper) to identify ports on a host that are open and waiting for connections. You will actually be using Zenmap, the graphical version of Nmap.

Exercise Diagram

This exercise uses the same diagram as the previous exercise.

Exercise Prerequisites

This exercise uses the same prerequisites as the previous exercise.

Exercise Steps

Warning: Do not attempt port scanning on a production network without written permission from your supervisor. Port scanning can be seen as a reconnaissance attack.

1. In order to run Nmap, you must install it along with WinPCap (Windows Packet Capture). Download Nmap from http://nmap.org/download.html and install it on your management workstation.

2. Click through the various prompts, accepting the defaults, to complete the installation. (The installation will actually install both WinPCap and Nmap.)

3. Start nmap by clicking on Start, mouse over All Programs, then mouse over Nmap, then click on Nmap –Zenmap GUI in Windows 7. In Windows 8.1, click on the Start button, then type "nmap" and press the Enter key.

4. Zenmap is the GUI version of Nmap, which will open when you choose nmap in a graphically-based operating system such as Microsoft Windows. In the Zenmap window, enter the IP address of your ASA's inside interface. Accept the default profile of "Intense scan", and click the button labeled "Scan". After a few moments, the results of the scan will be displayed in the Nmap output window.

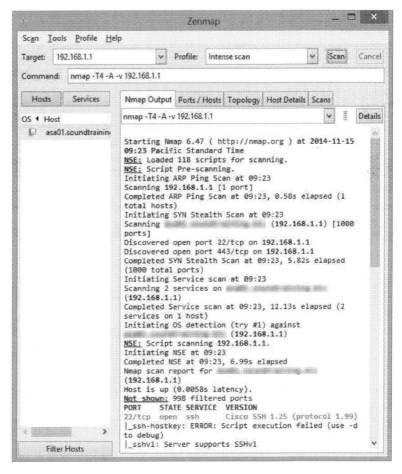

Figure 208:
An Nmap scan

5. Wait a few more minutes and Nmap will display information about any services it finds on the targeted host. Most likely, you will only see ports 22 (ssh) and 443 (https) open. You'll also be able to see information about the device itself including the version of ASDM.

6. If you are working with a partner, connect to the same VLAN as his/her management workstation and perform the same scan against that computer. Have your partner try disabling the Windows firewall on his/her computer and try the scan again. Compare the results. You should see many different services open after disabling the firewall.

For more information about using Nmap, visit http://nmap.org/book/.

For a lot of examples of Nmap scans, visit http://nmap.org/book/man-examples.html.

Now that you have made additional changes to your configuration, back it up using the procedures learned previously:

```
ciscoasa# copy run tftp://192.168.1.5/config _ filtering.txt
```

CHAPTER 11:
Configuring Transparent Mode

"Man will always find a difficult means to perform a simple task."

—Unknown

Understanding Transparent Mode

A Cisco ASA Security Appliance can operate in either routed mode or transparent mode. In routed mode, the appliance acts as a layer three device and the inside and outside interfaces have different IP addresses and are on different subnets.

Figure 209:
The difference in IP configuration between routed and transparent mode

Routed Mode
Inside
192.168.1.1/24
Outside
12.1.2.3/30

Transparent Mode
Inside
12.1.2.3/30
Outside
12.1.2.3/30

In transparent mode, the appliance acts as a layer two device. The appliance has a single IP address and the inside and outside interfaces are on the same subnets. Reasons to configure an appliance in transparent mode include:

- It is simpler to add a transparent firewall to the network than one operating in routing mode since there is no need to modify the existing IP addressing design

- Transparent firewall (layer 2) can pass certain types of traffic blocked by a routed firewall (layer 3)

- Routing protocol adjacencies

- Non-IP traffic, such as MPLS and some legacy protocols

A security appliance operating in transparent mode is not visible to most network scans and thus is less susceptible to intrusion attempts.

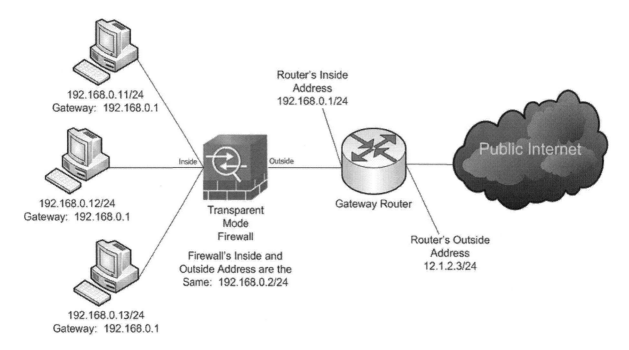

Figure 210: A security appliance operating in transparent mode in a network.

Hands-On Exercise 11.1:
Viewing and Changing the Mode

Exercise Diagram

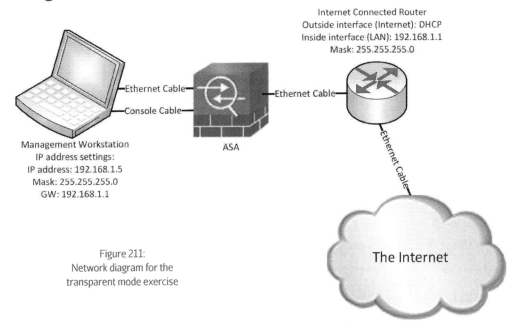

Internet Connected Router
Outside interface (Internet): DHCP
Inside interface (LAN): 192.168.1.1
Mask: 255.255.255.0

Ethernet Cable

Console Cable

Ethernet Cable

Ethernet Cable

Management Workstation
IP address settings:
IP address: 192.168.1.5
Mask: 255.255.255.0
GW: 192.168.1.1

ASA

The Internet

Figure 211:
Network diagram for the
transparent mode exercise

Exercise Prerequisites

The following exercise will erase your ASA's configuration. Make a full backup of the configuration before proceeding.

Watch the Video

There is a video on my YouTube channel in which I demonstrate the following procedures. Watch the video at http://youtu.be/Tv8Vag4eVdo.

Exercise Steps

You must first enable transparent mode on the firewall. Before executing this command, ensure that you have a good backup of the existing configuration. This command will obliterate the existing configuration.

1. In configuration mode, execute the command firewall transparent:

```
ciscoasa# conf t
ciscoasa(config)# firewall transparent
```

2. Next, assign physical interfaces to VLANs using the switchport access command and enable the physical interfaces with the no shutdown command:

```
ciscoasa(config)# interface Ethernet 0/0
ciscoasa(config-if)# switchport access vlan 2
ciscoasa(config-if)# no shutdown
ciscoasa(config-if)# interface Ethernet 0/1
ciscoasa(config-if)# switchport access vlan 1
ciscoasa(config-if)# no shutdown
```

3. After configuring the physical interfaces, you must configure the VLAN interfaces by giving them names and assigning them to the same bridge-group:

```
ciscoasa(config-if)# interface vlan 2
ciscoasa(config-if)# nameif outside
INFO: Security level for "outside" set to 0 by default.
ciscoasa(config-if)# bridge-group 1
ciscoasa(config-if)# interface vlan 1
ciscoasa(config-if)# nameif inside
INFO: Security level for "inside" set to 100 by default.
ciscoasa(config-if)# bridge-group 1
```

(Notice that the ASA automatically assigns security levels based on the names inside and outside. If you choose to give the VLAN interfaces different names than inside and outside, you will have to manually assign a security-level of 100 to the inside interface and 0 to the outside interface.)

4. Now, you'll configure the management IP address through the Bridge Virtual Interface (BVI):

```
ciscoasa(config-if)# interface bvi 1
ciscoasa(config-if)# ip address 192.168.1.240
```

(Notice that I didn't explicitly assign a subnet mask to the BVI's IP address. The ASA can assign a default mask based on the class of the IP address. Since 192.168.1.240 is a Class C address, the ASA automatically assigns a 24-bit mask of 255.255.255.0. If you're using something other than a default subnet mask, you can specify it in dotted-decimal notation following the IP address.)

5. The transparent mode configuration is now complete and the ASA will pass traffic. If you want to use the graphical ASDM (Adaptive Security Device Manager) to manage the device, you must enable the HTTP server and specify which hosts are permitted to access the ASDM with the following commands:

```
ciscoasa(config-if)# http server enable
```

```
ciscoasa(config)# http 0.0.0.0 0.0.0.0 inside
```

The first command does what the syntax implies, it enables the server. The second command permits any host connected to the inside interface, regardless of its IP address, to use the HTTP server. You might want to narrow the address range by specifying either your network address (in this example, it would be 192.168.1.0 255.255.255.0) or the host address of your management workstation.

Postlude

Congratulations, especially if you've actually worked through all the exercises in this book. That was a lot of work for you and you'll find that the work will pay off. I encourage you to go back and repeat some of the exercises, just to help you remember the procedures. (Repetition helps move the concepts and procedures you learn into long term memory.)

Consider pursuing certification, whether Cisco, CompTIA, Microsoft, LPI, or any other technical certification. I attended a seminar on the Linux boot process once in which the instructor commented that the more you know about one operating system, the more you know about them all. I absolutely believe that. Even if you don't pursue certification, be sure to attend seminars and workshops, watch educational YouTube videos, read more books, and work to develop an unquenchable thirst for knowledge.

My technical blog is www.accidentaladministrator.com where you'll find configuration guides, tutorials, and ideas about information systems and technology.

Set up test labs using tools like VirtualBox (www.virtualbox.org), GNS3 (www.gns3.com), or purchase used gear so you have a place to play and experiment. That's part of the fun of IT. We're geeks, after all. We love tech! (At least most of the time.)

Finally, remember that life success is not defined by technical expertise, but by being a well-rounded decent person. Get out from behind that monitor and broaden your horizons. Play music, paint, golf, go for walks, take a class, just do things to expand your life experience.

Work on being as kind and compassionate a human as you are a highly skilled and competent IT pro. Check out my blog at www.compassionategeek.com for some ideas.

Thank you for reading my book. You have my best wishes for tremendous success.

Peace.

APPENDICES

Appendix A:
Security Fundamentals

- The Elements of Security
- Vulnerabilities, Threats, and Attacks
- Security policies and the security process
- Defense in Depth

Network security is an extremely broad topic encompassing multiple facets. In order to effectively secure your network, you must consider factors including physical security, hardware security, operating system security, application security, and user security. It is important to realize that an effective security plan includes many different aspects and that there is no "one-size-fits-all" security plan.

The Elements of Security

The elements of security, although broad, can be broken down into four fundamental elements: availability, authenticity, integrity, and confidentiality.

Availability

Availability is the assurance that needed resources can be effortlessly accessed by appropriate end users.

Integrity

Integrity is the assurance that resources and communications have not been secretly altered between the source and the destination.

Confidentiality

Confidentiality is the assurance that resources and communications have not been mistakenly disclosed to unintended third parties.

Authentication

Authentication is the assurance that the individuals who are parties to communications or resource access are who they say they are.

Implementing the Elements of Security

Implementation of the elements of security takes place at multiple layers within a security infrastructure. The layers include the corporate security policy, physical security, user authentication, encryption and access control, and auditing and administration.

Figure 212: A security pyramid

Corporate Security Policy

The corporate (organizational) security policy is a road map that codifies the organization's expectations of security. It articulates where, on the continuum that is network security, your organization wants to exist. For example, at one extreme is a computer system that is totally unsecured. It has no passwords required for access and no restrictions are placed on any of the resources it contains. It is extremely easy to use (at least initially!), but totally non-secure. At the opposite extreme is a system encased in concrete disconnected from any and all networks. It is very secure, but unusable. Your organization must make determinations as to acceptable levels of risk, acceptable ways in which end users can use network resources, an auditing policy, and a disaster recovery plan. A written corporate security policy also provides security for IT staff in the event of a security incident: It allows IT staff to show that they implemented security procedures as directed.

Physical Security

Physical security such as locked doors or locked equipment racks is paramount to all other security configurations. In the absence of physical security, all other security measures can be easily compromised.

User Authentication

User authentication is the process by which users are identified and their identity is verified. Authentication is the first part of AAA (Authentication, Authorization, and Accounting). There are three factors that are used in authentication: Something you know such as a password or a PIN, something you have such as a smart card or a SecureID, and something you are such as a thumbprint or a retina scan. In most networks today, single factor authentication such as the combination of username and password is used to identify a user. Increasingly, security-conscious organizations are requiring two-factor authentication such as a smart card and a PIN. Obviously, the use of more authentication factors results in a greater level of security.

Encryption and Access Control

Encryption and access control are used to implement the confidentiality aspect of security. Access controls implemented through access control lists and entries provide protection for resources stored on network devices such as servers. Encryption provides protection for resources and communications once they leave the network device or in the event of a physical compromise of such a device.

Auditing and Administration

Auditing provides a means of reviewing what happened within a system. Administration is the ongoing process of performing security scans, mitigating any discovered vulnerabilities, and retesting to ensure mitigation and discover new vulnerabilities. It includes the use of management and monitoring tools as well as physical inspection of network infrastructure and devices.

Vulnerabilities, Threats, and Attacks

Vulnerabilities

Vulnerabilities are places within a computer's hardware, its operating system, or its applications that allow some form of unauthorized access or operations. Computers are simply machines that follow sets of instructions. They do not know the difference between authorized and unauthorized instructions unless they have a set of instructions telling them how to make such a distinction. Due to the sheer volume of lines of programming instructions in modern operating systems and applications, it is probably impossible to accurately and thoroughly audit all programming code for every error and/or omission. Such errors and/or omissions will eventually be discovered and possibly exploited by attackers. Part of the job of the security administrator is to anticipate such attacks and implement systems that act as barriers to the attack. The paradox is that, as a security administrator, you must anticipate the unanticipated.

Threats

Threats can be divided into two categories:

- **Structured Threats**—Structured threats are those that attack specific targets and are planned in advance. Structured threats are the most difficult to defend against due to their focused and persistent nature. Effective mitigation involves identifying the source of the threat and involving law enforcement or other authorities to disable the attacker.

- **Unstructured Threats**—Unstructured threats look for targets of opportunity. Attackers implementing such threats perform ping sweeps and other generalized scans to identify potential targets and, when one is found, escalate the attack by probing that target for various vulnerabilities.

Attacks

There are three broad categories of attacks:

- **Reconnaissance Attacks**—Reconnaissance attacks are a form of an unstructured threat that scans systems and networks looking for possible points of further attack.

- **Access Attacks**—Access attacks exploit discovered vulnerabilities to enter a system or a network. Upon successfully gaining access, an attacker might copy, modify, or destroy data, alter network resources including permissions and other access rights, or surreptitiously plant malicious code for future use.

- **Denial of Service (DoS) Attacks**—DoS attacks are designed to prevent access to network or system services by interrupting operations. DoS attacks frequently flood the target with more data than the target can process, thus forcing the target of the attack to either slow or shut down. In either case, a successful DoS attack prevents users with legitimate rights to access resources from accessing said resources.

Performing a Risk Analysis

Performing a risk analysis helps you make good business decisions about the type and extent of security to implement. In order to perform a realistic risk analysis, ask yourself four questions:

- What is the value of the data you wish to protect?

- What would it cost to restore or repair it?

- What is the cost of lost work and downtime?

- What is the potential cost of lost revenue?

Once armed with that data, you can proceed to quantify the cost of security breaches over a period of a year. Then, you can make informed decisions about an appropriate level of investment in security. For example, if your calculations tell you that the combination of lost time and resource access over a year's time is only $4,000, it makes no sense to invest $50,000 in security measures. If, on the other hand, you can mitigate such losses with a $600 investment, your decision becomes easy.

Quantifying the Cost

This simple formula will help you quantify the cost of security breaches. You can then compare the cost of breaches with the cost of various security implementations.

- S.L.E.: Single Loss Expectancy

- A.R.O.: Annual Rate of Occurrence

- A.L.E.: Annual Loss Expectancy

  - SLE x ARO = ALE

219

Types of Attacks

Targeted vs. untargeted attacks

Attacks fall into one of two broad categories: targeted and untargeted attacks. Untargeted attacks are things like a ping sweep looking for targets of opportunity. Untargeted attacks tend to be the easier of the two to defend against. Often, if reasonable security measures are in place, an untargeted attack will simply not discover your system and will move on to another opportunity. Targeted attacks tend to be a much greater challenge in terms of defense. A targeted attack is looking for something specific such as a customer database with credit cards, corporate marketing plans, or other sensitive information. A targeted attack could also be perpetrated by a disgruntled employee looking to interrupt network services. When measures are taken to block a targeted attack, the perpetrator often will continue to attack using different and sometime stronger measures. Targeted attacks are best dealt with by identifying the source of the attack and taking legal action to stop it.

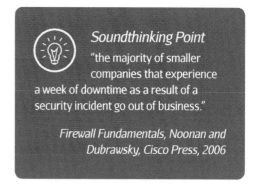

Soundthinking Point
"the majority of smaller companies that experience a week of downtime as a result of a security incident go out of business."

Firewall Fundamentals, Noonan and Dubrawsky, Cisco Press, 2006

Denial-of-Service Attacks (DOS)

Denial-of-service (DOS) attacks are used to interrupt network access. Legitimate users cannot gain access to resources such as file shares, printers, and databases. A common method of conducting a DOS attack is to flood the target system(s) with so many requests that it simply can not handle them and slows down, shuts off, or reboots. Some of the methods used in DOS attacks include:

Application-Level Floods

Application-level floods are often caused by a buffer overflow attack. A buffer overflow is an error in programming which cause memory access exceptions and program termination, or in the event of the user being malicious, a possible breach of system security.

Distributed Attacks

Distributed attacks occur when many systems flood a target simultaneously. Such attacks are often orchestrated using "zombies" (compromised computers centrally controlled by the attacker).

ICMP Floods

ICMP floods can take several forms, most notably a Smurf attack in which the attacker floods a misconfigured network with a broadcast PING. The fake the source IP address as that of the victim and the resulting responses to the victim impair its ability to function.

An ICMP flood occurs when the attacker send the victim an overwhelming number of PING packets, often using the ping –f command. The victim is not only overwhelmed by the packet flood, but bandwidth saturation also prevents legitimate traffic from going to or from the victim.

Nukes

Nukes are specially crafted or malformed packets. Older operating systems such as Windows 95 cannot handle such packets and may lock up.

Peer-to-Peer Attack

A peer-to-peer attack takes advantage of a vulnerability in common P2P protocols to force clients to disconnect from their peer-to-peer file sharing hubs and to attempt to connect to the victim's server instead. Web servers, for example, can handle hundreds of simultaneous connection attempts, but when faced with thousands or tens of thousands of simultaneous connection attempts, they may shut down.

SYN Flood

In a SYN flood, the attacker sends multiple TCP SYN packets from a spoofed address. The receiving systems responds with SYN/ACKs, but since the sender's address is forged, the receiving system gets no response. It is left with multiple half-open connections (called embryonic connections) and eventually shuts down.

LAND Attack

LAND attacks are similar to SYN floods, but they use the target's IP address with an open port as both source and destination. The victim replies to itself continuously until it crashes.

Malware and malicious content

Malware and other malicious content include viruses, worms, Trojan horses, and compromised websites. Javascript and ActiveX vulnerabilities can be used to plant malicious code on a victim's computer.

Social engineering

Social engineering occurs when an individual is tricked into revealing confidential information. Such an attack might occur when the attacker poses as someone from the IT department performing maintenance and requests the victim's username and password for "testing" purposes.

Spyware and compromise of personal information

Phishing attacks are a form of social engineering. They occur when the attacker creates a website bearing a close similarity to a genuine site and tricks the victim into revealing personal information such as credit card numbers or social security numbers.

Keyloggers can be planted by Trojan horse programs to record the victim's keystrokes and gain personal information.

Understanding Defense in Depth

Defense in Depth in the Military

Defense in Depth is an ancient military concept in which multiple barriers were erected to protect a city or a fort. The idea is that each barrier provides not only a challenge to an attacker, but also an opportunity for the defender to stop an attack.

The 18th century fortress of San Cristóbal is an example of Defense in Depth. Covering 27 acres, San Cristóbal was built to protect San Juan from a land attack. Its "Defense-in-depth" meant that each part of the fort was supported by one or more other parts. The fort has several barriers, each of which must be compromised in order to complete a successful attack. Each barrier also provides an opportunity to repel an attacker, or delay a successful attack. (As a point of interest, San Cristóbal was an active Army fort as recently as 1961. Today, it is under the jurisdiction of the US National Park Service.)

Defense in Depth in a Network

Figure 213:
Viewing Defense in
Depth graphically

Policies and Procedures

Security policies, organizational procedures, user education, backup and restore strategy

Physical security

Guards, locks, physical access control

Perimeter security

Firewalls, routers with access lists, VPNs

Internal network

Network segmentation (VLANs, subnets), network-based IDS

Server hardening

Hardened OS, authentication, auditing

Firewall on host

Inbound TCP/IP port and address control

Virus protection

Installed and maintained virus protection software

Intrusion prevention

Zero Day attack protection

Patch management

Security updates

Data security

Endpoint security, secure communication paths such as SSL, TLS, IPSec

Application and Data

Strong passwords, file/directory permissions

Appendix B:
Understanding Security Contexts

Security contexts provide a means of creating multiple virtual firewalls on a single physical appliance. Security contexts are used when it is desirable to provide firewall services for different clients with different configurations for each client.

Each security context is stored in a separate file which can be stored in Flash memory or on a TFTP, FTP, or HTTP server.

Context names can be up to 32 characters in length, are case sensitive, and can contain letters and numbers and a hyphen.

Decisions about how to route traffic flows are based on what characteristics of the traffic flows are unique to a context. Characteristics used in routing determinations are source interface (VLAN) and destination address.

A security appliance can be configured to operate in either single or multiple context mode with the *mode* command:

```
ciscoasa(config)# mode ?

configure mode commands/options:
  multiple   Multiple mode; mode with security contexts
  noconfirm  Do not prompt for confirmation
  single     Single mode; mode without security contexts
ciscoasa(config)# mode ▮
```

Figure 214:
Viewing the current mode

You can view the current mode with the command show mode.

Changing from one mode to another requires a reboot.

Admin Context

When operating in multiple mode, security appliances use a special context to manage the system interfaces and all other contexts configured on the appliance. This context, called admin context, is stored in a file called admin.cfg which must be located in Flash memory.

Soundthinking Point

Security contexts are not supported on the Cisco ASA 5505 Security Appliance.

When operating in admin context, you have control over all other contexts. For that reason, it is recommended that access to admin context be limited through AAA local database configurations with access controls.

Context admins can be configured for each individual context. Such administrators have admin rights only over their own context and cannot affect system resources or other contexts.

There are two parts to a security context:

- System configuration of the context—This defines various aspects of the context including the context name, its VLAN, interfaces assigned to the context, and the name and location of its configuration file.

- The context configuration file—This contains the configurations including firewall policies, interface configurations, and other parameters unique to the context.

Creating a Context

Use the context command to create a new context and move into context configuration mode:

```
ciscoasa(config)# context client01
Creating context 'client01'... Done.
ciscoasa(config-ctx)#
```

Figure 215: Creating a context

Appendix C:
The Tools of the Book

- Abyss Web Server: www.aprelium.com
- The Java Applets: www.realapplets.com
- KiwiSyslog: www.kiwisyslog.com
- Nmap: www.insecure.org
- PuTTY: www.putty.org
- Solar Winds TFTP Server: www.solarwinds.net
- TeraTerm: http://sourceforge.jp/projects/ttssh2
- TFTPD32: http://tftpd32.jounin.net

Appendix D:
Table of Figures

Index

BOOKS
For I.T. Professionals
from author Don R. Crawley

Ubuntu Linux Server for Accidental Administrators®: An Illustrated, Step-by-Step Configuration Guide

Packed with more than 30 easy-to-follow interactive exercises, loads of screen captures and lots of step-by-step examples to help you build a working router from scratch, *Ubuntu Linux Server for Accidental Administrators®: An Illustrated, Step-by-Step Configuration Guide* is easily the most straight-forward approach to learning how to configure a build an Ubuntu Linux server. You'll learn the nitty-gritty on user and group management, the Linux help system, monitoring, search and scheduling tools, BIND DNS, remote administration, and more.

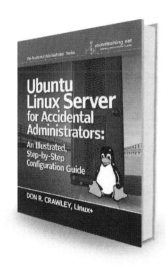

ISBN: 978-0-9836607-4-3
Available in Spring 2015 in paperback and Kindle editions through Amazon and other channels.

Tweeting Linux: 140 Linux Configuration Commands Explained in 140 Characters or Less

In it's first edition, this guidebook is a straight-forward approach to learning Linux commands. Each command is explained in 140 characters or less, then examples of usage are shown in screen captures, and details are given when necessary to explain command usage. You'll see the most commonly-used commands plus a few gems you might not know about!

ISBN: 978-0-98366-071-2
Available in paperback and Kindle editions through Amazon and other channels.

The Accidental Administrator®:
Linux Server Step-by-Step Configuration Guide

Packed with 54 hands-on, step-by-step exercises and 185 graphics including screen captures showing you exactly what you should be seeing on your own screen. It's the most straight-forward, visual approach to learning how to configure a Red Hat/CentOS Linux server, filled with practical tips and secrets learned from years of teaching, consulting, and administering Linux servers. There's no time wasted on boring theory. The essentials are covered in chapters on installing, administering, user management, file systems and directory management, networking, package management, network services, security, performance monitoring, management tools, and more.

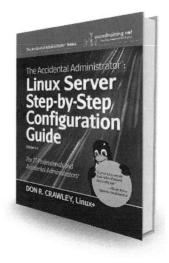

ISBN: 978-1453689929
Available in paperback and Kindle editions through Amazon and other channels.

The Accidental Administrator®:
Cisco Router Step-by-Step Configuration Guide

Packed with more than 30 easy-to-follow interactive exercises, loads of screen captures and lots of step-by-step examples to help you build a working router from scratch. Easily the most straight-forward approach to learning how to configure a Cisco router, this book is filled with practical tips and secrets learned from years of teaching and consulting on Cisco network devices. All the essentials are covered in chapters on installing, backups and restores, and TCP/IP. You'll learn the nitty-gritty on subnetting, remote administration, routing protocols, static routing, access-control lists, site-to-site VPNs, network address translation (NAT), DHCP, password recovery and security. There's even an entire chapter on the new Internet Protocol version 6 (IPv6)!

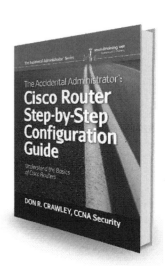

ISBN: 978-0983660729
Available in paperback and Kindle editions through Amazon and other channels.

soundtraining.net
accelerated IT training

THE COMPASSIONATE GEEK:

How Engineers, IT Pros, and Other Tech Specialists Can Master Human Relations Skills to Deliver Outstanding Customer Service

Now in its third edition, *The Compassionate Geek* is the definitive guide for delivering amazing customer service to customers and end-users. Filled with practical tips, best practices and real-world techniques, *The Compassionate Geek* is a quick read with equally fast results. Each chapter contains a reflection and discussion section to help improve customer service skills. Inside are lots of personal stories and examples of mistakes made and lessons learned in addition to an entire chapter on overcoming personal and professional obstacles. All of the information is presented in a straightforward style that can be understood and used right away. There's nothing foo-foo, just down-to-earth tips and technical support best practices learned from years of working with technical staff and demanding customers and end-users.

Available in both paperback and Kindle editions!

BOOK DETAILS

Author:
Don R. Crawley

Categories:
Business & Economics/
Customer Service

Distribution:
CreateSpace

Publisher:
soundtraining.net
Box 48094
Seattle, WA 98148
(206) 988-5858

Official release date:
November 1, 2013

Number of pages: 224

Book size: 6 x 9

ISBN: 978-0983660736

Made in the USA
San Bernardino, CA
02 February 2019